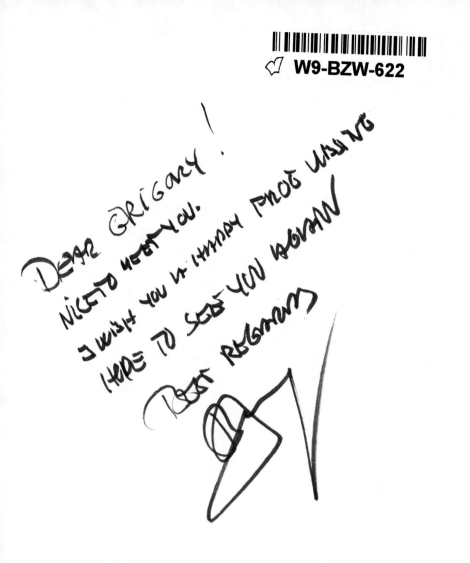

Dear Grigory!

Nice to meet you.

I wish you a happy food making

Hope to see you again

Best Regards

W9-BZW-622

Dare to Kiss
the Frog

Finn van Hauen
Bjarne Kastberg
Arlene Soden

Dare to Kiss the Frog

Transform Values into Action
by Rethinking Control

Savage PRESS

Box 115, Superior, W I 54880 (715) 394-9513

Dare to Kiss the Frog
Transform Values into Action by Rethinking Control

© Copyright by Scandinavian Knowledge Development, Inc.
March, 1999.
All rights reserved.

Authors: Finn van Hauen
       Bjarne Kastberg
       Arlene Soden
Cover: Nicolas Remming
Layout: LYMI - Broendbyoester

The font used in this book is Cheltenham.
Printed at Bang Printing, Brainerd, Minnesota.
1. English edition
ISBN 1-886028-37-0
Library of Congress Registration Number: 98-061711
Published by Savage Press

Scandinavian Knowledge Development, Inc.
1822 Minnesota Avenue
Duluth, MN USA 55802-2436
Phone 1-218-722-8217

Scandinavian Training Design A/S
Vodroffsvej 40
DK 1900 Frederiksberg (Denmark)
Phone +45 35 37 00 99

E-mail:
✔ Finn van Hauen: fvh@std.dk
✔ Bjarne Kastberg: bk@std.dk
✔ Arlene Soden: atsoden@uslink.net

**The authors frequently conduct board
retreats, strategic planning sessions,
team building, and other development
activities based on this and related topics.**

Dare to Kiss the Frog

Have you ever experienced an inability to accomplish projects or implement new organizational strategies due to a lack of commitment and motivation?

Has your organization had difficulty in the market that could not be explained by simple logic?

If you want to harness the power of transformation, you must examine your own beliefs about the most fundamental issue of leadership—**control.**

Kissing a frog is not a very pleasant proposition when you first consider it. However, the desire for the end result can cause you to take the risk. As a manager, so it is with examining your own beliefs about the use of control. Perhaps it's not appealing at first glance— but it can lead to incredible results!

To "rethink control" is to begin the transformation. The "prince" you get is insight about the following:

✔ why rules and behavioral control do not create responsiveness; and why we consequently have to rethink our concept of control
✔ how to recognize the hidden factors within your organization that support change, adaptability, innovation and commitment
✔ how to relate purpose, values and beliefs to everyday actions
✔ how to rethink reasons for performance problems
✔ how to clarify communication

This knowledge will increase the effectiveness of your life and your organization—

without even practicing!

Dare to "kiss" by:

- ✔ Investing an evening to read this book, and
- ✔ With the insights gained, reorganize some of your beliefs about leadership and control.

It's all in your head!

Does it sound too simple to you? Are promises like this all too common in business literature?

Well, that is the first of your beliefs to reorganize.

Complicated things need not be complicated to explain. We believe even the deepest thoughts should be expressed in simple, everyday language.

The concepts we offer you here are simple, yet subtle.

We are sure you will find the journey exciting and thought provoking. Confront yourself with your own values and beliefs. In this process, you will find most of the answers within yourself – including answers you did not even know you had.

Finn van Hauen   Bjarne Kastberg   Arlene Soden

Contents

Introduction

You may be a reader who learns non-sequentially and browses in the chapters. If so, we recommend you resist browsing until you have read the three first chapters. That's where the general outline of ideas is presented. The rest is more suitable for browsing.

Here is an outline of the contents:

Chapter 1 defines the nature of beliefs. It describes the framework for understanding how beliefs are formed and reformed. It describes the relationship between strategic management and the supporting culture.

Chapter 2 shows the relationship of values to behavior. This is the basic model for how to understand effective values-based leadership.

Chapter 3 describes values paradigms that organizations adopt to deal with the outside world. They are the keys to diagnosing organizational culture, belief and values.

Chapters 4 through 10 are about the fundamental applications of the model. Practical tools to implement an aligned culture are presented.

Finally, **Chapter 11** sums up reorganized beliefs about leadership in an aligned organization. There are a few final ways to test it out as well.

There are lists of definitions and literature references at the end of the book.

Chapter 1

What is this all about?

1.1 What is a Belief?

This book is about "kissing the frog"—examining and reorganizing our beliefs about the use of control as managers. Why is that important?

Our own beliefs and values are factors that we do not always readily recognize. Nevertheless, they are the most fundamental determinants of behavior. The assumptions we make comprise our perception of reality.

Every time you introduce a new management model in your company, a set of beliefs will follow. Introduce "teamwork" and assumptions about cooperation and trust come along. Introduce the idea of a learning organization, and assumptions about the value of learning and win/win concepts are added. Not recognizing the hidden beliefs and values in your organization might lead you to introduce concepts that have absolutely no support—and no chance of getting it. We will go deeper and deeper into that understanding in this book, building your insight piece by piece.

Most of the time the explanation for someone's behavior is rooted in his or her beliefs and values. If you are interested in bringing about change, you must start with recognizing your own beliefs. You must also master the skill of "surfacing" the beliefs of others.

The initial question to ask is: "What is a belief?"

> A patient arrived at the doctor's office and stated his conviction that he was a corpse. Not a very productive thought, of course, but this fellow was thoroughly convinced of it.
>
> After consideration, the doctor thought to ask the patient if corpses could bleed. The patient replied, "No."
>
> The doctor then—to prove her point—triumphantly took a needle and punctured a small hole in the patient's arm. Out came a tiny drop of blood.
>
> "Oh!" exclaimed the patient. "I didn't know that corpses could bleed!"
>
> ~ adapted from Robert Dilts, et. al.

> Two co-workers were discussing the day's work. They began to talk about a new team at the office that was forming for a project.
>
> "...because, of course, everyone on a team is equal," one stated.
>
> The other worker was incredulous. "That's not true! A team has many different positions—first string, bench warmers, special players. There is always a definite pecking order."

Through what we say and do, we expose our beliefs about **how things are.** Some of our assumptions may be highly productive—others the opposite.

For example, imagine that in your youth you participated in a team and it did not work out very well. You were even embarrassed. It is likely that you formed your first opinion about teams at that time. "Teams do not work" started to grow in your mind. You perceived more and more examples to support that thinking until one day it was there—a genuine belief: "Teams do not work. I have seen it a hundred times."

CREATING BELIEFS

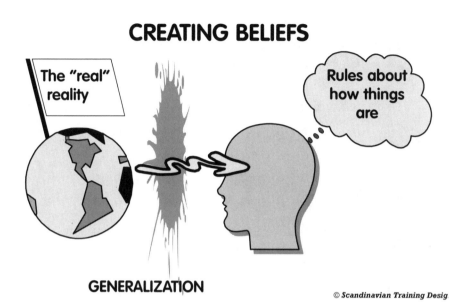

The "real" reality

Rules about how things are

GENERALIZATION

© Scandinavian Training Desig.

It works the other way as well. You deliver a successful speech and the opinion starts to grow, "I am good at speeches!"

Is it true that teamwork does not work because you had a bad experience? And is it true that you are a good speaker because you were successful once? No one can tell from just that.

Beliefs are created by generalization of successful or unsuccessful experiences in your life. They are rules you feel need no further proof about how things are.

1.1.1 Surfacing Beliefs

Let's increase your ability to bring beliefs to the surface and recognize them. Try this:

"He is always late. He has disrespect for his colleagues."

What has to be true for a person who makes that statement? Yes, he or she has to believe in some sort of rule that being late is equal to disrespect. This might be true—but then again it might not be. The only way to know is to ask.

> **To uncover the rule, ask yourself, "What does this person have to believe to make that statement?"**

Try it once more.

"If we stick to broad issues, we will probably not have a disagreement."

What kind of belief would lead someone to say this? A belief that some sort of disagreement exists!

To do this requires practice. You will become better and better every day. At last you will be an expert!

1.1.2 Changing Beliefs

To create learning, you must have the ability to break limiting assumptions that have grown into beliefs.

First, let's examine what really goes on inside someone's head when he or she breaks with a previous belief.

Here is an example. Imagine that you believe you **are** a person that avoids conflict. A conflict arises. Because you have long ago generalized that you are someone who avoids conflict, your immediate reaction is a low recognition of your own ability to address it.

A helpful approach is to "think about your thinking"—to look at your own thinking process in perspective. Take a "helicopter view" and ask yourself what kind of generalizations led you to believe you could not deal directly with a conflict.

Let's assume you remember some instances when you actually avoided conflict. You might then ask whether a few examples are enough to generalize from. You might even remember that in some other cases you handled conflict with great success. Finally, you might reach the conclusion that in some cases you avoided con-

THE RE-FORMATION OF BELIEFS

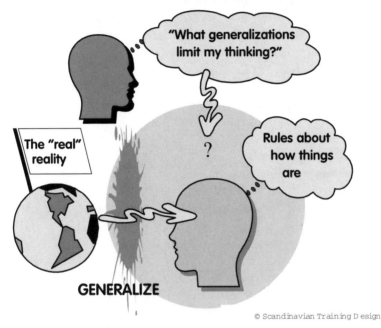

"What generalizations limit my thinking?"

The "real" reality

?

Rules about how things are

GENERALIZE

© Scandinavian Training Design

flict and in other cases you did not. Perhaps this actually makes you an extremely effective person.

Now you can resume your normal position thinking about the upcoming conflict with a much more productive belief: I **am** a person that deals well with conflict. I have the ability to choose either to address or to avoid conflict!

Several techniques can be used to bring about recognition of beliefs. Here are some of them:

The first suggestion is to **surface the belief.** State the assumption out loud. That in itself could have an amazing effect. In the above example about disagreement, *"If we stick to broad issues, we will probably not have a disagreement,"* you could ask:

"Do you think there are things we do not agree on?"

By asking the question, you invite the other person to think about his or her own thinking. This is exactly what is required to uncover an unspoken belief. You will then get cues to discover whether there is a particular issue behind it or simply a generalization about always disagreeing with others.

The second suggestion would be to **create a situation** where the original assumption proves untrue. This opens the possibility for some other, more productive, assumption to take its place.

This is one of the principles of team building. Creating an experience of good teamwork breaks old assumptions that teams are not worthwhile. A well executed team building simulation brings out the assumptions participants usually make without conscious consideration.

The third way to surface beliefs is to **ask.** Asking questions without offering one's own opinion is the heart of good coaching. When asked thoughtful questions, people normally come to recognize their own assumptions—very often changing them on their own without further ado.

You sell hammers and a customer comes in and asks for one. He then asks, "How much will I earn using this hammer?"

It is not easy to give a precise answer. You might say something like, "I have a friend who saved several dollars building a deck." or, "I have a customer who saved more than a thousand dollars building his own house."

Are those convincing answers? No. The problem, of course, is that we do not know this person's objectives for buying the hammer.

In the same way, it is difficult to give a precise answer to the question, "How much will I earn implementing a learning organization or values-based management?" without defining the context.

The fourth suggestion would be to offer some other explanation based on logic. (Like the doctor who tried to convince the patient that he was not a corpse). Some people are convinced by pure logic and let go of previous assumptions on that basis alone.

The fifth suggestion would be to use a **metaphor or analogy.** Offer a story that illustrates the problem in another way. Here is one:

> It is easy to tell an experienced lumberjack from a beginner. When a log jam occurs, the beginner goes down to the river and begins to move logs one by one until the jam clears. It is often exhausting, unrewarding work.
>
> The experienced lumberjack, in contrast, first climbs a tree to determine which log is causing the jam. Only then will he go down to the river. He pulls out the one or two logs that are preventing movement, and once more the flow of work continues.
>
> The same process is useful in organizational leadership—stopping to get perspective and insight can save many hours of wasted effort!

The sixth suggestion would be to **break the automatic response** of the assumption. Offer a new pattern. That is, expose the assumption as less practical behavior. Could it be that someone always assumes that Christmas parties have to end up in chaos to be truly fun? Then create a different pattern for "fun." Make the previous thinking inconsistent with the newly experienced reality.

> *To break a limiting belief, you have to "think about your own thinking" and replace unwarranted generalizations that you have made in the past.*

1.1.3 Special Belief Patterns

Have you ever heard the phrase: "If we allow that—we will never be able to draw the line between what's right and wrong."

CHANGING BELIEF PATTERNS

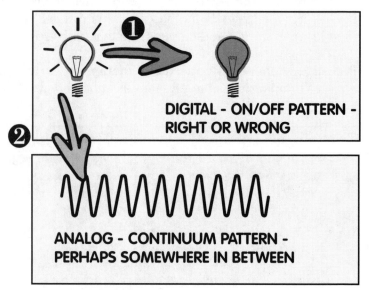

DIGITAL - ON/OFF PATTERN - RIGHT OR WRONG

ANALOG - CONTINUUM PATTERN - PERHAPS SOMEWHERE IN BETWEEN

This is what we call a distinct digital pattern. It's either right or wrong. Some people display such a pattern. They do not have gradations in between.

Others organize their beliefs as "perhaps." We call it an analog pattern. Those are people who accept a continuum of possibilities. "I assume this to be right, but in this particular situation we must consider a number of options."

When you meet people with digital patterns you may try to persuade them to the opposite viewpoint. That is, you try to use the strategy similar to 1 in the figure. Sometimes it might be better, though, to consider strategy 2.

Moving yourself or another person from a digital to an analog pattern may in the long run give you much more personal flexibility than moving a particular digital viewpoint.

It's time to try it out!

Try our entire
bath tissue
facial

PAPER
NOT F
PLEASE RE

www.marcals

Consumer A
Marcal Man
Elmwood Pa
Please include packag
©2009 MARCAL

hium Recycled
AVE 1 MILLION TREES®

VING TREES SINCE 1950

1.2 The Strategic Environment

Let's come back to the initial questions.

Have you ever experienced an inability to accomplish projects or implement new organizational strategies due to a lack of commitment and motivation?

Has your organization had difficulty in the market that could not be explained by simple logic?

Most certainly you have experienced this. Haven't we all? Let's examine what this is about.

We have all learned a lot about strategic management—planning, calculating, marketing, producing, budgeting and all of those issues. Many of us have accepted that running a business or an organization is dependent on being good at all of these tasks. Having the ability to run an organization depends on assigning jobs to everyone and creating a master plan from which actions can be determined.

The basic belief associated with strategic management is that cause and effect governs our lives. A proper input and a proper process create the proper output. **You can control things if you are smart enough.**

However, we all know this does not apply anymore to many of the tasks that business must perform today. Typical examples could be:

A single bank in Japan breaks down, and one year later the catastrophe has affected the entire world.

New applications of technology evolve every minute. Some of them, called "killer apps," make old businesses irrelevant overnight while creating new opportunities.

In addition, planning and control are based on the assumption that **things can be managed by rules and regulations,** by controlling behavior. But in an environment of change and unpredictability, you will never have enough rules to cover every situation.

One common assumption was **that a company could be led to a state of static equilibrium.** Today we know that we will never find a stable situation that our business can rely on.

> *The traditional belief in controlling <u>cause</u> <u>and</u> <u>effect</u> has to be reformed. If you want to create adaptability, you must be able to manage uncertainty.*

1.2.1 The Hierarchical Organization

Many organizations still draw their organizational chart as a hierarchy. The belief that accompanies this is again having direct control over a certain amount of subordinates.

But is the assumption of hierarchy a productive one?

Take a simple system like traffic. Assume that you want to control traffic in a hierarchical way. Every morning commuters call the central traffic control system that registers data in the central traffic computer.

When it is time to start your commute, the computer telephones you and you get in the car. The computer now takes over the driving, controlling the flow of traffic in every street and alley throughout the whole country.

Sometimes the computer experiences a glitch and traffic stops for some time–everywhere. The system has very low redundancy, the ability to function even when some part of the system fails.

Occasionally, streets are under repair or perhaps a pedestrian falls in the street. There is no way for the computer to receive information about these events. Consequently, things go wrong. Cars are driven across fallen people or into repair holes. The rigid system adapts very poorly to daily changes in conditions.

Fortunately, things do not actually work this way. In fact, traffic flow is controlled by the collective decisions of millions of independent minds—those people who drive by a few simple principles: *Take the less crowded route, don't bump into the cars in front of you, don't drive over pedestrians, stay in your lane,* etc.

This is called *hive intelligence.* The totality of millions of drivers in their vehicles collectively operate this complex system by very few rules. Though comprised of multiple single entities, each autonomous unit influences the other through feedback loops according to internal rules.

> *The traditional belief in controlling people has to be reformed. If you want to create adaptability, you must have self-controlled people in the organization.*

1.2.2 Redundancy

Many reengineering efforts are aimed at eliminating redundancies. Business Process Redesign is one. This makes the organization "lean and mean." Right?

What's the belief here? **The fewer resources you put in, the more efficient you get.**

In arenas that are stable and predictable, this kind of efficiency makes sense. In the turbulence of the real world, however, a reliance on minimalist efficiency can spell disaster.

Look at the structure of complex systems. They do not work like the minimalist model. Any one traffic accident has no effect on traffic nationwide. As motorists choose detours to avoid the problem, the system needs only to adapt within a local area until more permanent repairs can be made. Alternate routes function as work-arounds for any obstruction to traffic flow.

The organization then must minimize the effect of errors by maintaining appropriate system redundancies. The system stays intact. When special opportunities arise, it is prepared to take advantage of them.

> *The traditional belief in controlling <u>efficiency</u> has to be reformed. If you want to create adaptability, you have got to have redundancy. You cannot have maximum efficiency AND adaptability.*

Do not mistake it. Redundancy does not mean having people as back-up doing nothing. It means providing for different ways to move on even if something breaks down. This keeps everyone productive.

1.2.3 Network Economics

Let's consider two relatively new companies.

✔ **www.amazon.com** This "little" company was almost nothing three years ago. Now it's one of the world's largest bookstores.
✔ **Microsoft** is the second most valuable company in the world.

They have achieved in a short time what many companies took a lifetime to accomplish. What have they done differently?

It's a new ball game called a "network economy." As we become increasingly connected, new rules come into play. You don't fill a bathtub one cup at a time. You look for the faucet. In marketing, this means create a path to your product or service and the world will buy your product by the millions.

Create a path to your bookstore, and people will find it. Create the operating system for your computer and people will buy all your other programs by the millions. In other words, make it easy to buy from you. Many companies prosper by just selling a path. There are costs to get on their server with references to your web page.

An additional example of this is mobile phones. From the telephone company's point of view, the ownership of the network increases exponentially through increased use. Therefore, it makes sense to sell the mobile telephones at rock bottom prices, even give them away, in order to increase the use of the real product they want to sell—the use of their network.

> *The traditional belief in controlling __networks__ has to be reformed. In a network economy, "control" means to create a path to your product. Make it easy for your customers to find and use your product.*

With a network economy, production facilities can be located anywhere. Your lawyer, your administration, your packaging and distribution, your server, your marketing—really any aspect of your operation can be geographically dispersed. The new game is to get the best people to do the job, wherever they are.

What matters in a network economy is the internal network of information and knowledge that you create and foster.

> A small company, The Official Airline Guide, collects information on flights from all over the world and publishes a World Wide Directory in book and in electronic form. Nothing really unusual, but it is known worldwide. This company was sold for $750 million—probably more than you can get for most airlines with planes, hangars and all.

In this scenario, value shifts from fixed assets to the creation of knowledge assets. Getting information is not difficult today—the value comes in the filtering of information to glean what is usable at the most useful moment possible.

> *The traditional belief in controlling __physical__ __assets__ has to be reformed. Controlling assets means to control __knowledge__ __assets__.*

1.2.4 Innovation

The last strategic issue to address is that you cannot force people to be innovative or make them commit to the business by traditional control.

Chaos, relativity and uncertainty are principles of physics that dominate more and more of our lives. You might argue that this has only theoretical application to daily business issues. However, creativity is one of those practical arenas where business must rely on more than logic. The rules of simple logic do not apply here. Any effort to apply it to organizations fails at some point.

Here is an example of this. You are reading this book. It's a book about belief systems and the issue of control. You are probably interested in those topics. But reading it might give you an unexpected insight into something else that is unrelated. It might also be a starting point for a conversation in which you create a lot of business in the year to come.

So, all logical results from reading this book are not specific and foreseeable. If you rule out all of these other factors in your organization, things become rigid and unable to adapt.

This is where FUN-phobia comes into it—the fear of not being serious enough.

> One of our clients told us that his math teacher used to say: "Stop laughing—math is no fun!"

When we conduct our seminars and workshops, we often work with the concept of "state." That is, we create a playful psychological environment that facilitates learning, openness, and low resistance. The response is overwhelming. People say that after three hard days they feel relaxed but amazingly filled up with new insight and learning. Our participants appreciate this state as being highly productive.

Yet, there are times when we encounter new customers who tell us: "We heard that you have a relaxed and playful atmosphere in your seminars. Just for your information, our management is not like that. They would like us to be serious all the time!"

One attractive aspect of not being too serious is the increased ability to innovate.

> *The traditional belief in __being serious__ has to be reformed. Controlling innovation means to create a playful culture.*

1.3 The Cultural Environment

Strategic management is the heart of business. Direct control still applies to many situations—there is no doubt about that. However, to cope with all of the changing circumstances that we just outlined, you have to re-create an effective culture in which to do business.

THE FRAME

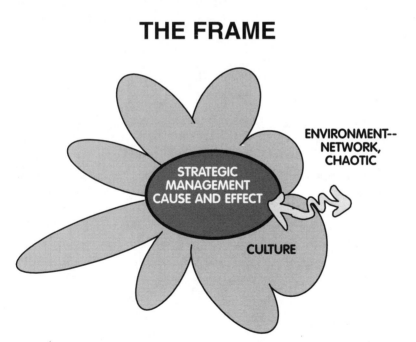

ENVIRONMENT--
NETWORK,
CHAOTIC

STRATEGIC
MANAGEMENT
CAUSE AND EFFECT

CULTURE

The culture of an organization is its collection of prevalent belief systems.

One purpose a culture should fulfill is **support commitment for the strategic issues** at hand. It has to support learning, creativity and good working relationships that permit high productivity. This is what chapter two is about.

The second purpose of a culture is to **create an effective interface with the outside world.** It has to enable you to cope with the external environment. It must address all of the apparent irrationalities and rapid changes. It must make your organization adaptable and flexible as a whole and on an individual level.

Look at the figure on the previous page. It shows the organization as an amoeba. The strategic issues are the nucleus, and the rest of the amoeba is the culture. The culture supports the nucleus with energy (commitment) and helps it adapt to the outside world. The culture supports the communication from the nucleus to the external environment and vice versa. This is addressed further in chapter three.

Let's return to the original questions:

Have you ever experienced an inability to accomplish projects or implement new organizational strategies due to a lack of commitment and motivation?

Has your organization had difficulty in the market that could not be explained by simple logic?

You may have overrated the ability to plan and control changes. Do you acknowledge the significance of creating an organizational culture to support your ideas? Let's look into how this can be done.

Chapter 2

Managing for Commitment

2.1 "But that isn't the real me."
Logical Levels of Change

Following a presentation, we had this exchange with a member of the audience.

"You work with people who want to change, right?" asked the person who had heard the presentation.

"Oh, yes," we answered.

"I want to change," she responded. She then continued, "Can you help me?"

"Yes, sure," we replied. "What do you want to change?"

"I want to..." and then a long descriptive explanation followed.

"You really have it planned well. Is any of it something you can already do?" we asked.

"Yes, of course." Then she continued with a long list of qualifications she possessed.

Then came the crucial moment—we questioned:

"If it's something you can do, why don't you start right away? Then you have changed!"

She looked at us as if she had approached the wrong group–and said while losing interest:

"But that isn't the real me!"

Let's look at that last statement.

What was she really saying? Why couldn't she change when she had the ability to do so?

Consider the model on the next page, The Logical Levels of Change, created by anthropologist Gregory Bateson. The theory we present to you is not the original theory from Bateson, but our own work based on his original ideas.

The model is drawn like a triangle. This is how Bateson originally created it. The model shows the five levels in which we express ourselves. **It's a triangle. The levels are linked hierarchically to each other. However, do not mistake it for Maslow's hierarchy of needs that you may know.** Do not associate any specific metaphoric idea behind it.

In going through the model, try to think of your work.

Environment refers to the surroundings in which we operate. *Where do you work?*

Instead of just answering with the company name, go a bit deeper. Where do you perform what you are paid to do? At home, in the office, at meetings?

Behavior is what we actually do. *What do you actually do?*
Once again, don't just answer with your position title. Go deeper. What is it you are paid to do? What behavior do you actually receive your paycheck to perform?

LOGICAL LEVELS OF CHANGE
FOR INDIVIDUALS

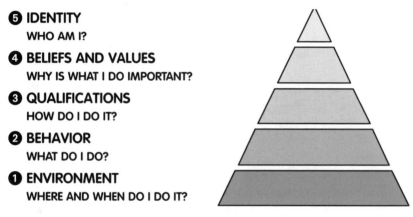

❺ IDENTITY
WHO AM I?

❹ BELIEFS AND VALUES
WHY IS WHAT I DO IMPORTANT?

❸ QUALIFICATIONS
HOW DO I DO IT?

❷ BEHAVIOR
WHAT DO I DO?

❶ ENVIRONMENT
WHERE AND WHEN DO I DO IT?

Qualifications are the abilities we possess to do what we do. *What enables you to do your work?*

What do you really use? It is not just factual knowledge. Include all of your internal strategies for getting things done.

Let's stop for a second. What is the "logical" part of the model? The logical part is that the levels link together. Nothing can really change in one level without affecting other levels. If you want changes on a particular level (such as behavior) you will get the best results if you also focus your efforts on surrounding levels as well (qualifications, values, identify or self-concept, and the environment).

Beliefs and values are the reasons you have obtained your qualifications. *What is important about having the qualifications you have and doing what you do?*

What brought you to the position in which you are today? What values and beliefs are driving factors in your life?

Identity is the person you believe you are. *What is your self-concept at work—having the values you just disclosed?*

If you find it difficult, ask yourself what you want to be said at your farewell party if you retire. Who is the person that carries those kinds of values, that is able to do that kind of work in the places you do it?

What is this really about?

Look again at the sentence: "But that is not the real me!" We asked about **behavior and qualifications.** She answered about her sense of identity. Her change problem was not one of qualifications, but one of identity. The new behavior did not match her self-concept.

People want all aspects of their lives to be consistent. We are uncomfortable learning and doing things that are not congruent with our identity or values.

> *Congruence is a desired state where all levels of an individual (or a team, a department, or an organization) are consistent and in harmony with each other.*
>
> *The fundamental key to motivation and behavior change is our drive for internal congruence—a consistency among the levels.*

If you introduce a change on levels of environment or behavior, it will succeed long term only **if** it keeps the person congruent **or** values and identity change accordingly.

2.1.1 Personal congruence

> Last year we had a large client and thousands of people in training. We had trained 33 managers in a "Train the Trainer" program to assist us with the job.
>
> We also introduced the model of Logical Levels of Change to

them. After one of the first training sessions, an employee came up to the Human Resource Manager for a discussion. He had just been introduced to the model the day before and concluded that his values did not fit into his current position. He wanted a change of job!

The Human Resource Manager was so overwhelmed by the effect of the course that he immediately created a solution with him.

Personal congruence is essential.

PERSONAL CONGRUENCE

Congruence is the primary motivating factor in daily work and in producing change.

2.1.2 The Mirror Test

People evaluate you on what they observe. Everyone has an opinion about what values and intentions are reflected by a given behavior. We refer to this as a "map of the world."

But this can lead to many false assumptions and wrong guesses about the intentions of others.

If you want to get behind behavior and find out what the "map" is— what particular values and intentions another person has—you have to ask. The number one question is:

How can it possibly be so?

If someone sits with arms crossed and looks down, is he offended? Is he sad? Is he bored? Is he cold and calculating? Maybe he is very interested, but tired. *One can only know by asking.*

Now comes the tricky part: *What kind of belief systems must you have to put that question to work?*

First of all, you must believe that there is a worthwhile answer, otherwise you would probably not ask. You must also believe the following:

> *To ask for the intentions behind a behavior you have to believe:*
>
> * *That the answer will improve the relationship with the person you ask, thereby making it worthwhile asking.*
>
> * *That there is probably a positive intention behind the (unusual) behavior.*
>
> * *That every person has his or her own unique "map of the world."*
>
> * *That it might be of value to know about the maps of others.*
>
> * *That you are not able to read minds.*

Reading minds is a favorite occupation for many people!

Carrying these beliefs with you is also your personal key to excellent communication. Whom would you rather meet: a person who asks about your intentions and values, or one who assumes he knows you and therefore judges you based on his own perceptions? Just think of it!

> I don't like that man. I am going to have to get to know him better.
>
> *— Abraham Lincoln*

Here is a story from Finn's family:

The Mirror Test

> Rikke, my 13-year-old daughter, came home one Friday angry and disappointed with Maja who apparently was not very nice to her.
>
> "Then you have a problem," I suggested. But no! She did not have a problem. Maja had the problem. She did not behave nicely towards Rikke.
>
> "Let's try the mirror test," I suggested. She curiously asked what that was.
>
> "Imagine Maja on Monday morning. She enters the bathroom, stretches out her arms, looks in the mirror and says:
>
> "Maja—beautiful girl—what a marvelous morning. What a tremendous week this will be. You'll do well. This is going to be great. But wait! I have a problem. I cannot behave well toward Rikke. I must solve that."
>
> Now Rikke did not agree with the last part. "No, dad. She would not say that."
>
> "OK," I answered. "Let's try you. What might you do?"

"Rikke—beautiful girl—what a marvelous morning. What a tremendous week this will be. You'll do well. This is going to be great. But wait, I have a problem. I have to meet Maja. Oh no."

"Yes, that's more likely," agreed Rikke. "You made your point. I have the problem, not Maja."

Monday evening I asked Rikke what action she took. She answered that as she had the problem, she approached Maja. Rikke asked about her intentions since she did not understand Maya's behavior. As it turned out, Maja did not mean to offend her—so they were friends again.

Asking the question, *"How can it possibly be so?"* can be a key to conflict management.

What you will notice is that much of the time:

People judge themselves by their intentions, but judge others on the basis of behavior.

I once complimented a good friend on his ability to listen. Getting a sheepish look on his face, he related this story:

He had taken a class on listening skills in college. The professor noted his fine abilities and commented, "Bob, you are doing a great job at making it *look* like you're listening. Now, what would make it even better is if you actually listened!"

All the techniques in the world won't work unless you match them with supporting beliefs.

—Arlene

In our presentation skills training courses we occasionally include a session by an image consultant. This session is designed to show

how style and color of clothes can influence our opinion about people. In the session there are a number of examples. Participants freely express their prejudices to everyone's great enjoyment. Some pictures actually show the same person in different clothes and demonstrate how assumptions about the person change drastically as a result.

The presentation shows how quickly we proceed from registering facts to drawing conclusions. It is sometimes as little as a fraction of a second. Our consciousness moves at lightning speed.

2.1.3 The Other Crucial Question

There is another important step in this process. If the primary change mechanisms are values and beliefs, nothing could be more important than to ask:

"What is important about that?"

In answering that question, people will give you clues about their primary motivation factors. Think about it. In sales situations, instead of pushing on to praise all the benefits of your product, one simple question would allow you to frame your sales discussion around precisely the things your customer values.

THE IMPORTANT QUESTIONS

"HOW CAN IT POSSIBLY BE SO?"

"WHAT IS IMPORTANT ABOUT THAT?"

By the same token, this same question would normally be considered to show interest and real concern—something that you want to convey both as a salesperson and as a leader.

In our workshops, we occasionally hand someone a pen and ask the person to "sell" it back to us. Often, he or she will begin by immediately explaining the features of this wonderful pen. They sometimes hit what we value about pens—but often miss the mark completely. Another way to proceed is for the person to ask the key question:

"What features of a pen are most important to you?"

They might even ask about the additional logical levels of behavior and environment. For example, "How and where do you use pens?" Once they have these answers, they can then "sell" us the pen more effectively! In addition, as a customer I am satisfied because my needs on all levels are being addressed.

If you forget everything else in this book don't forget to ask:

* *"How can it possibly be so?"*

* *"What is important about that?"*

This will give you keys to creating commitment, congruence, and true understanding.

2.1.4 What Are Values?

How do you define a value? Many people have difficulty in expressing a definition. An example of a value statement might serve us well.

When asked about your important values you might respond, "I value challenge in my work."

If we keep on pressing and ask again, "What is important about challenge?" the next answer might possibly be in this vein: "Challenge gives me satisfaction."

Be sure to notice this. It shows that the value represents a personal state, "satisfaction."

> *Values represent states we prefer to be in. To recognize if something is of value is to examine the state it puts you in.*

2.1.5 Context - Different Identities

The logical levels depend highly on context. We have core values that are deeply rooted and global but we also have some that are dependent on circumstance.

If you were to describe your identity as a family member, it would most likely not be the same as a description of yourself at work.

In a public office where we conducted a large organizational development project, we realized that roles for employees in the central administration differed highly during the day. The situation called for roles from controlling, leading, consulting, and gathering information to that of project participant.

To enable everyone to understand not only the values implied by each role but also the potential value conflicts, we asked each of them to draw up the triangle model for each role. They answered the questions for each role and level.

That exercise created a lot of insight and was a prerequisite for creating a new respectful culture between the central administration and employees out in the field.

2.2 Organizational Alignment

Collective systems also carry an identity and system of values and beliefs. In the same way that the model applies to motivation and change for individuals, it also applies to groups and organizations.

LOGICAL LEVELS OF CHANGE FOR ORGANIZATIONS

❺ ORGANIZATIONAL IDENTITY
WHO ARE WE?

❹ ORGANIZATIONAL VALUES
WHY IS WHAT WE DO IMPORTANT?

❸ ORGANIZATIONAL SYSTEMS AND KNOWLEDGE
HOW DO WE DO IT?

❷ ORGANIZATIONAL PROCESSES
WHAT DO WE DO?

❶ ORGANIZATIONAL ENVIRONMENT, LOCALLY AND GLOBALLY
WHERE AND WHEN DO WE DO IT?

To some degree, individuals working within a system must align their logical levels with the organization if there is to be a good working "fit."

Alignment occurs when a single entity brings its Logical Levels into sync with the next higher system. (Examples: Individual to a team, team to a department, or department to the rest of the organization.)

Organizations that have alignment of shared values increase employee commitment, confidence and achievement.

As we will show in the rest of the book, visions, knowledge management, teamwork, personnel appraisals, hiring decisions and promotions are all areas where this model of alignment can be applied with tremendous power.

INDIVIDUAL ALIGNMENT TO THE ORGANIZATIONAL LEVELS

Note that the alignment process involves values. When people align, sometimes they mistake behavior for values. Just copying behavior is not alignment and does not create the desired results.

> *Despite the parents' effort to teach children good manners, they tend to behave like their parents anyway.*

2.2.1 Robbery of Meaning from Public Life

Most behavior-oriented management techniques are designed to bring conformity and efficiency to even greater heights. In a mechanistic world, individual differences and inputs are problematic to organizational efficiency and are seen as interfering with progress. An unintended effect of this emphasis on behavior alone, however, is that the personal meaning of our work is relegated exclusively into a private arena. Not much in the way of our hopes, dreams, traditions, and passionate pursuits are addressed in our public life.

The absence of individualism in organizations has turned into a "robbery of meaning" from public life. Most of what we call our *life* is outside of the system.

More than a search for balance, many want integration. Today's workers are seeking not just a place to work, but a place to belong.

2.2.2 Values and Virtuality

In addition to being co-authors, we own a consulting company. Arlene is based in Duluth, Minnesota, USA, and Finn and Bjarne are based in Copenhagen, Denmark.

We work in a "virtual organization" over a great distance. Because we believe that detailed control is not the key to making such a partnership work, we make some conscious decisions about using the higher levels of identity and values.

For example, when negotiating our formal legal agreements and developing initial business plans we were only able to schedule three days to physically meet together. Instead of turning directly to the piles of legal papers, we began by each explaining our perspectives and values. We explored each of the logical levels. Questions such as, "Who are you?" (identity) "Why do you want to do this?" "What is most important to you?" (values) "What do you bring to the group?" "What do you expect to learn?" (qualifications) "What do you want to do?" (behavior) and "Where do you want to do it?" (environment) were explored. This discussion lasted a full day.

In the remaining two days, the framing of the legal paperwork went much more smoothly because of our understanding of each other's perspectives and visions of the future.

When conflicts arise or decisions must be made quickly, we return to our core values for direction.

In times of change, alignment with values is the compass.

2.2.3 Different Levels of Values

We agreed in section 2.1.4 that values on a personal level are a state we want to be in. But what happens on an organizational level?

Values in organizations are expressed in three layers.

THE VALUES LEVELS IN DETAIL

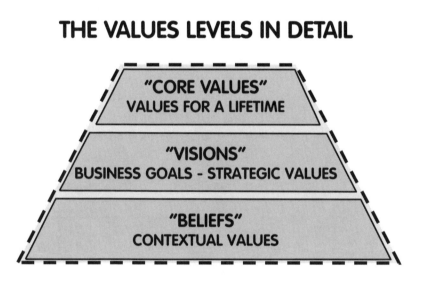

"CORE VALUES"
VALUES FOR A LIFETIME

"VISIONS"
BUSINESS GOALS - STRATEGIC VALUES

"BELIEFS"
CONTEXTUAL VALUES

Core values are the values on which the organization relies—often for decades—that are linked closely to the core business. In James Collins' book, *Built to Last,* he states preserving core values is one element that distinguishes lasting businesses from ordinary ones that come and go. When all else changes—keep the core. These values are not to be sacrificed for short-term expedience.

Strategic business values are the values that are often reflected in the business plan. "We want to develop this market or technology in the next two years." These are actually "visions" in a business sense.

Contextual values are day-to-day beliefs. These are the rules about what's important in each context. These are the criteria we apply when choosing among solutions.

In a generalized sense, values are likewise states the organization wants to be in.

Let's consider for a moment the statement that people must leave if they do not align with organizational values.

The bottom line is that people must leave if they cannot support the company's **core values.** There is much more latitude on the other levels of values. People might commit themselves to some of the business goals and be brilliant employees even if they do not share all of the goals. A mismatch of core values should be so uncomfortable that it causes a reaction like a bad virus—an "organizational sneeze!"

Contextual values may differ highly from situation to situation. Strong organizations benefit from an appreciation of differences on this level. By encouraging diversity of perspective, the organization benefits from the emergent capabilities of each one, allowing for individual congruence.

One work group discovered its contextual values were quite different between two members in particular. One person sought creativity and defined it as, "a chance to do things in a different way each time."

Another group member sought order and described it as "finding predictable, systematic ways to get things done." There was potential for a good deal of conflict.

They confirmed their core value of **service** to the customer and each other in the work group. By clarifying their differing contextual values, the two work group members made conscious decisions about when each of their preferences should be used to benefit the group.

2.3 Managing the Levels

Until now everything has been common sense. But one thing that is characteristic about common sense is that it's by far not common. Let's examine common management behavior.

As mentioned before, one might assume that learning something would be the basis for a new behavior. This is not so. Knowing the logical levels, we know that values and belief systems must change as well to apply the new knowledge.

In classical organizations, the focus is on the managers' own learning. The more clever and bright the managers were, the better. Management's learning alone, however, does not create change in the organization.

What happens when managers learn new things yet don't change their values? They tend to go home and force everyone else to adopt the new behavior, yet they do not adopt it themselves.

The classical belief system about management is that management requires direct control of things. It assumes that management

MANAGING THE LEVELS
CLASSICAL CONTROLLING

MANAGER'S VALUES	ORGANIZATIONAL VALUES
❶ MANAGER LEARNS	ORGANIZATIONAL LEARNING
❷ MANAGER CONTROLS	❸ ORGANIZATION BEHAVES

THE MANAGER

THE REST OF THE ORGANIZATION - THAT IS, THE EMPLOYEES

knows what's good for others and that others are probably better off if told what is good for them.

The belief is that sharing power may be too risky considering that management still has responsibility if something goes wrong.

Managers continue to directly control others with whatever they learn. The tools they have learned are incentives, punishment, directions, budgets, memos, and competitions. These are all motivational factors on a behavior level, only minimally touching on some of the higher logical levels.

In the figure on the previous page the classical controlling sequence is:

❶ Manager learns.
❷ Manager controls.
❸ Organization behaves.

Champy claimed in *Reengineering the Corporation* that managers are the chosen few who do not change in large organizational development projects. As a result, nothing is really changed. There is just a new model—a new management fix. Many want to change, but few actually do it.

What we suggest managers do is illustrated on the next page. The values-based sequence is:

❶ Manager learns.
❷ Manager develops others.
❸ Organization gains an understanding of values and learning.
❹ Organization finds the best behavior.

This is a crucial place to examine your own beliefs. What we propose is that management work indirectly with behavior—creating organizational behavior by influencing organizational learning processes and values. Can you accept this kind of indirect influence?

MANAGING THE LEVELS
INFLUENCING VALUES AND LEARNING

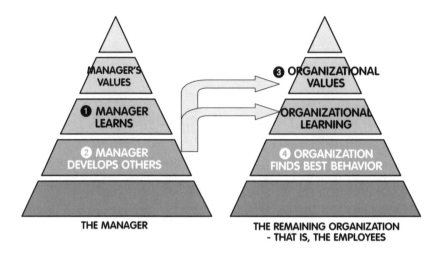

One day in a large health care organization that cared for older adults, the summer heat became so intense that one client fainted in the cafeteria line. Others were also having extreme difficulty moving about. When complaints were made, the employee in charge said nothing could be done. After hearing about the situation from an angry customer, the top administrator contacted the direct service employee. The worker explained that a rule had been set that no one could spend over $20 without a supervisor's approval. The supervisor was on vacation. (Yes, the OK was given to obtain a $22 fan by the top administrator!)

Are your customers fainting for lack of your employee's autonomy?

Let's make a wonderfully simple conclusion about management styles. Take a look at the figure on the next page. This provides new insight into all of the different management ideas talked about in the last decade.

> **The Learning Organization is leadership based on the logical level of qualifications.**

> **"Values-Based Management" is leadership based on the logical level of values.**

DIFFERENT MANAGEMENT STYLES

MANAGING THROUGH VALUES -
VALUES-BASED MANAGEMENT

MANAGING THROUGH LEARNING
THE LEARNING ORGANIZATION

**MANAGING THROUGH
CONTROLLING BEHAVIOR -**
CLASSICAL MANAGEMENT

Managing this way may be described as:

> **Follow me—I'm right beside you.**

Have you ever heard someone say:

"Management is never around, but they often cause havoc in the daily business! What could they be thinking?"

Strange? Not really. The interpretation might be as follows:

"Management values are not known to us. We do not know what their intentions are, but they are certainly messing up on directing our behavior level all the time."

Do not misunderstand our purpose here. Depending on the context, managing on a behavioral level can at times be the best approach. Certain safety measures or industry regulations call for specific behavioral approaches. It may be useful for quality assurance and production control, for example.

Values-based leadership is being able to use other levels **in addition to** direct behavior control.

Once when speaking to a large group of people, I began the speech by asking, "Does anyone here wonder why they really need to become a learning organization?" There was a show of hands in agreement.

Later on, when I explained this idea of managing on different levels, I asked:

"Do any of you enjoy being told what to do and having your behavior controlled?" Not one hand was raised!

Then I asked:

"Do any of you at this moment realize why becoming "a learning organization" may be important to you?" Again, there was a show of hands!

Motivation, change, adaptability, flexibility, complexity, and networking are not regulated by traditional behavioral control. These areas are the domain of congruence and alignment on higher logical levels.

What we have discovered is that many managers feel uncomfortable managing on higher levels. Values-based leadership is being able to manage behavior when appropriate, and working on higher levels when commitment, innovation, and motivation are the focus.

> It's a daily task of management to tempt the employees to do their very best.
>
> *Jette Pio Trampe,*
> Managing Director of Social Institutions, Frederiksborg County, Denmark

MOTIVATED BEHAVIOR IS DRIVEN BY VALUES AND QUALIFICATIONS

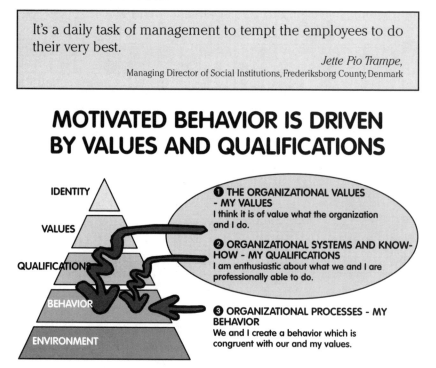

"Manipulating" people is what happens when your actions do not correspond with your intentions. You must always be prepared to honestly explain the relationship between your behavior and intentions.

> A department manager returned to her office after meeting with the staff. "I have such great ideas for how they could do things better—now if I can just get them to think the ideas are theirs!"

Creating ownership of any introduced change is one of the classical problems in management. Change initiatives, visions, new business processes and the like are not "owned" by everybody, and management fights vigorously to create that desired ownership.

By managing on higher logical levels, **ownership is automatically created** through the organization's own values and learning. This, in turn, creates the desired behavior.

> At a university, "Don't walk on the grass!" signs were placed on the lawns. The response was that students picked up the signs and placed them in garbage cans—and kept walking on the grass. New signs were posted that said, "Give earth a chance!" Students walked on the sidewalks.

2.3.1 An Example

One of our clients owns a hospital system. Their plan, along with other hospitals in the area, was to save money on internal service departments.

DISRUPTING CONGRUENCE

One of the competitive hospitals went straight to the behavioral approach. They told the employees who transported beds that from now on they were going to clean, also. As you can imagine, this was not the kind of work these people regarded as their choice. They did not have any sense of identity attached to it. The result was that they walked off the job. The hospital scrambled for replacements.

We were more conscious of values with our client. We introduced the concept of self-managing groups to accomplish all of the unskilled work that had to be done.

We then offered them a new values system for their work.

✔ An opportunity for *personal development*—(specific educational sessions)
✔ *Self-management*—the *freedom* to plan their own work
✔ *Equality*—partnership with other departments and negotiating the service to be delivered
✔ Social *belonging*—a working context having close relationships with peers

No one left. They groaned, but they stayed. Six months later, no one would dream of going back to the old system.

Organizations change when new and more attractive values are offered.

As we began working with a group of managers that had experienced much conflict and turnover, we asked them to draw how they saw themselves. The results were an indication of what was holding them back:

• One person drew a new car to represent himself. Eggs were being thrown at the car.

• One person drew a barnyard where the manager was in the center being pecked to death by chickens.

• One person drew a spotlight on the manager with a group of judgmental onlookers surrounding him.

We then asked the managers to find a new metaphor for their **identity** that would match what they desired to be true about themselves as leaders. They discussed this and returned with the metaphor of being "quarterbacks" on a football team. We followed through by asking, "What is important about that?"

Several key **values** were identified. Next, we looked at the required **qualifications** for someone to be able to carry out those values. From that, we identified what **behaviors** would be consistent for a leader who had those values. We considered how the new concept of their identity and values fit in with the organizational **environment.**

Changing the self-concept and identifying the associated values enabled these departmental leaders to obtain qualifications and take on the behaviors consistent with their new self-concept.

2.3.2 Why is it Difficult?

Generally speaking, it should be easy, but it rarely is. Let's look at factors that can be overwhelming to managers who would like to make this shift in style.

Obstacle number one: you have to acquire the skills to do it.

Have you mastered a learning management style? Have you any knowledge about how to teach and how to influence people?

Many managers do not have sufficient professional tools of control to do the job in this way. They are good at planning, budgeting, selling, buying and so on. They are not, however, especially qualified in the roles of mentor, trainer, or coach that enable others to develop their abilities.

Obstacle number two is the risk of failure.

Maybe you are not so self-confident. Up until now, you have been successful in what you have done. Then you realize you **must** do something else to continue having success. Can it really be true? Is the world changing so rapidly that you have to learn these new skills? Or would it be sufficient to continue doing what you have always done? If you try to change, is it likely that someone else in the organization would be better at it?

Then there is obstacle number three—the issue of rethinking your understanding of control and to begin using the concepts of congruence and alignment.

Imagine that you have done all this. What happens if the resulting behavior of your employees is not exactly as you envisioned? Can you live with that?

It's really the whole idea—employees finding better methods on their own than the ones you wanted to implement! You have to live with it—even be proud of it. You have to have the same feeling of success as the teacher who eventually sees his students succeed on their own.

I was a senior manager in a company that introduced a new system for arranging client files. I directed the staff in my region to begin using this new system. The idea was met with much resistance. After listening to their insight, I asked them to come up with what they thought would be workable. Their method was so "user-friendly" the whole company adopted their system instead—saving much time and money.   –Arlene

---

Obstacle number four is time.

Giving rules is *initially* less time-consuming than discussing values and learning new qualifications. Time is scarce; in front of you is the enormous investment that has to be made before results begin to pay back dividends of time in abundance. *Nothing will give you more time in the end than self-reliant employees.* Are you ready for the up front investment?

Obstacle number five is that in addition, your employees may question your abilities!

Some years ago Finn was a new managing director in a company he purchased. After a month, one of the managers

---

came up to him and said, "This is not going to work."

"What is not going to work?" he asked curiously.

"The way you can't decide," he said. "Apparently you are not able to make decisions."

"What do you mean?" Finn asked.

He replied, "You always ask us about our opinions, our preferences, our qualifications. We are accustomed to a manager who can tell us the rules we have to operate by. If you really want to know what I feel is important, I think you should behave like a 'real' Director; one who gives orders, exerts control and keeps the employees in check. Someone who takes advantage of the privileges every Director should have."

Some people do try to keep things as they are, and your employees are probably no different. They will need to have an understanding of their new role as well.

Obstacle number six is that all this might not be congruent with your self-concept.

Refer back to the initial story: "Is it really me?"

At the many courses we conduct, we have worked with a large number of senior managers from the social services sector. On an assessment test of management style, results show that most of them score low on team orientation.

"Why is this?" they ask. "We are all from the social sector. If anyone understands teams it must be us."

We respond, "We do not believe so. Many of you became managers because you didn't like to be in individual contact with your clients. Most of you didn't want to work in the operating teams."

Managers who want their organization to work in teams are not necessarily team players themselves. The way to handle this is to expose them to some practical, positive experiences with teamwork. They then realize the advantages of change.

Obstacle number seven is another hard-dying concept of the struggle between "profits and results vs. process."

Some years ago when Finn was relatively new in business, one of his colleagues came up to him and asked him about TQM (Total Quality Management), on which he was an expert. For an hour he explained everything the person needed to know for the next meeting. For Finn, the session seemed to be over, but then his colleague asked: What about the process?

Finn was a little confused. What process?

Then the colleague explained to Finn that all he had explained up until now was the content—how things were meant to be. Now he was concerned about how he should implement it. How were they going to learn this? How could they carry it out?

Finn realized that he had only provided him with half of the answer. You surely recognize that many times you know the answer but do not know how to explain it.

What we learn here is that all communication consists of both content and process. We need to decide **what is to be said** and especially **how it is to be said** if we want to get results.

Controlling by congruence and alignment is a *process* concept of control. It's handling the logical levels beyond behavior—to influence behavior in the process. It's based on "bio-logic," not a precise deterministic "cause and effect" relationship.

But many managers find that uncomfortable.

Some find it easier to ask, "What's in it for me?" If they do not find the precise cause-and-effect over a short span of time, they do not believe it's going to happen.

> *It's difficult to change for many reasons: lack of qualifications, high degree of risk, accepting others' solutions, investing the time, keeping credibility,*

accepting new leadership values and learning to treat processes as equally important as results.

Can you truly say:

"Oh, yes, that's really me."

2.4 Leadership Roles

If it is not controlling behavior, what is the job of a leader? What are the implications of shifting a considerable amount of what constitutes leadership into managing values and qualifications?

Perhaps you have read many leadership and management books. Each time something has been added to your concept of how to be a leader. Like a Christmas tree, every year you buy additional ornaments to put on it, but you never throw any out.

Try to think of it this way: How much can you remove and still have a Christmas tree? When will it turn into just a pine or spruce tree that for some reason was put inside your house?

One of the decorative balls is "planning." Can that one be removed? Yes, probably. *There are certainly many fine leaders who are not great planners.*

Another trinket on the tree is "a detailed understanding of financing." Can it be removed? Yes. The company controller can cover that one.

But no one can remove the star called **direction.**

Figuratively or literally, leading someone to another place means knowing where that place might be. Otherwise, it's not leadership. It means creating support for the vision.

One more glowing ball has to stay. It's absolutely necessary for any leader to **create understanding** about the tasks and the job to be accomplished. If only one person knows the goal, how can any sense of collaboration or contribution take place?

Lastly, the manager has to **walk the talk**—or at least "stumble the mumble!" This is the star on the tree. This means living the values of the company as well as his or her own values. Be personally congruent. There is no way out of it. Remember, people judge you on behavior, not on your intentions. (Section 2.1.2) The people around you are a mirror of what you convey.

These three truths are developed in the following table.

No.	Leadership Role	Which consists of...
1	**To communicate direction; the shared vision.**	• Making sense and giving direction • Showing **congruence** between visions and means to achieve them • Creating support and acceptance • Creating **alignment** with people's personal visions
2	**To create an overall understanding of the system**	• Creating an understanding of the whole. Create **congruence** in a broad sense • Creating cooperation and learning across boundaries • Create alignment among the interest groups
3	**Walk the Talk**	• Exhibiting the organization's values • Showing **congruent** personal behavior • Creating productive belief systems and discarding limiting beliefs • Creating **alignment** with the employees' values and the organization's values

Simply put, managing the logical levels of change and taking on these leadership roles is what values-based management is all about.

> *Management has to be focused on congruence, alignment and on shared values and vision.*
>
> *This means taking on management roles that facilitate these processes in the organization.*

A manager's role in this environment is not much different from that of an athletic team coach. She develops a strategy. She trains her players so they have a shared understanding of the common goal, of the game itself, and the game plans they will use. The coach develops the team's knowledge about the opponent's tactics. Managers these days aren't always present when and where the game is played. Actually, they haven't been there for a long time!

The coach's most important job is to create players with open minds; players who can learn from a situation not only individually, but also collectively. Innovative players are needed who can spontaneously create new strategies and tactics to exploit opportunities without having to ask for permission first.

2.5 Rethinking Control

What you will see in your organization in years to come is people who want to be in congruence with themselves and proud to be in alignment with an organization. This means a breakdown of traditional command and control and increased non-hierarchical networking in a virtual workspace.

To deal effectively with this environment, you must rethink control —and lead by congruence and alignment.

> *The rethinking of control is needed when organizational systems do not lend themselves to direct behavioral control.*

Increasingly, leaders understand the need to appeal to the higher logical levels of others. It means focusing on relationships, communication and other qualifications in addition to those directly related to behavior and performance.

> ### The "soft stuff" is the "hard stuff."

Most management books impart various skills and techniques. Readers are ready to evaluate the value of the content on its immediate effect on the bottom line. This whole "tool" point of view—management as a technical discipline—can easily lead a manager to overlook the fact that management is not the practice of all of these maneuvers and skills. They may be a means to an end but are not ends in themselves.

This is truly how you focus on the bottom line. If you work with process you may have to wait for several years, but the final effect has the potential of a revolution. You can compare it to training for years for the Olympics to achieve the ultimate result.

> Examples of the differences can be seen in two comparable organizations: Amnesty International and Greenpeace.
>
> Amnesty International has been led for years by involving unpaid volunteers on principles of congruence and alignment. Today it is more influential and has more members than ever before.
>
> Greenpeace is run by hierarchical leadership. It is declining in participation and membership support.

Looking at the response of volunteers exposes the long term results of each type of leadership.

The figure on the next page summarizes it. We must move from managing only on the levels of behavior, competence and values to managing on all levels. This encompasses the whole culture with congruence and alignment.

THE EVOLUTION OF MODERN MANAGEMENT

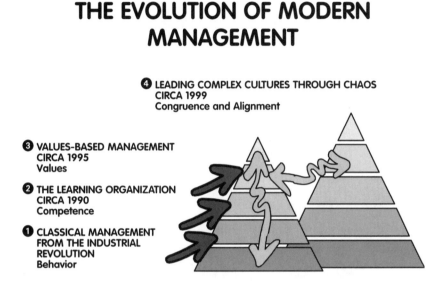

❹ LEADING COMPLEX CULTURES THROUGH CHAOS
CIRCA 1999
Congruence and Alignment

❸ VALUES-BASED MANAGEMENT
CIRCA 1995
Values

❷ THE LEARNING ORGANIZATION
CIRCA 1990
Competence

❶ CLASSICAL MANAGEMENT FROM THE INDUSTRIAL REVOLUTION
Behavior

2.6 Creating the Culture

If your kids ambush you the moment you come home from an exhausting day at work and cry in your tired ears, "Can we go to a movie tonight?" the answer is probably, "No."

On the contrary, if they ask you an hour later when you have unwound a bit, they may have much more probability of producing their desired result.

What we are talking about is "state."

> *State is a prerequisite for communication, learning and change to take place at all.*

If you don't have the appropriate "state" you can save yourself the trouble of even attempting to communicate.

> *Creating an environment for congruence and alignment in the organization is the most important factor for the sharing of values and for learning and development processes to take place.*

Chapters four through ten develop some of the essential conditions for creating a "collective psyche" that will establish the right state in the organization. Each chapter outlines some of the beliefs that accompany the approach.

2.6.1 The Seven Disciplines

Here is a general introduction of these requisite conditions.

CREATING AN ENVIRONMENT FOR CONGRUENCE AND ALIGNMENT

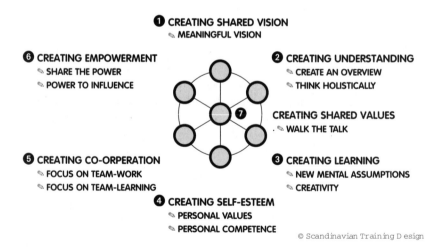

❶ CREATING SHARED VISION
    ✎ MEANINGFUL VISION

❻ CREATING EMPOWERMENT
    ✎ SHARE THE POWER
    ✎ POWER TO INFLUENCE

❷ CREATING UNDERSTANDING
    ✎ CREATE AN OVERVIEW
    ✎ THINK HOLISTICALLY

CREATING SHARED VALUES
. ✎ WALK THE TALK

❺ CREATING CO-ORPERATION
    ✎ FOCUS ON TEAM-WORK
    ✎ FOCUS ON TEAM-LEARNING

❸ CREATING LEARNING
    ✎ NEW MENTAL ASSUMPTIONS
    ✎ CREATIVITY

❹ CREATING SELF-ESTEEM
    ✎ PERSONAL VALUES
    ✎ PERSONAL COMPETENCE

© Scandinavian Training Design

1. Creating Shared Vision

No one hurries along the pathway without a purpose. If purpose is absent, we just stroll. Creating vision is about making sense and about alignment with organizational business values. Too many vision statements do not make sense or result in commitment. They are just words—not words to live by.

2. Creating Understanding

Without an understanding of the whole picture, you begin to feel frustrated and tend to lose a sense of accountability. You need to see yourself as a valuable part of the organization. You need to see how what you do "fits in," how you align.

3. Creating Learning

People sometimes carry mental assumptions—belief systems that are counterproductive to learning. Creating learning is about making beliefs visible to each other and making conscious choices. Creating learning is about substituting limiting beliefs with more productive assumptions. People are surprisingly unaware about learning processes, even their own learning. Creating a culture of learning presupposes mutual respect for differences in perception and learning style.

4. Creating Self-Esteem

People do not produce effectively or change while emotionally distressed. Try to imagine someone arriving at the office, having just left a "war zone" at home, feeling badly about themselves, saying: "How I look forward to learning something new today!"

Creating self-esteem is taking care of congruence in the upper personal logical levels. You will see how it fits the model.

Creating self-esteem is a fragile thing. As a manager you cannot just order some to pass around. You have to understand how it's created on individual and organizational levels. You have to understand how you might damage it without even being aware.

5. Creating Cooperation

A basic definition of an "organization" is a group of people interacting coherently for a common purpose. Values discovery, alignment and learning processes are predominantly linked to cooperation. If people do not feel a part of it, these favorable processes will not happen.

Creating teamwork is about creating competence in handling social relationships and learning in teams.

6. Creating Empowerment

Humans abhor a vacuum of influence, especially when it comes to using what they have learned and living out their own values and beliefs.

Creating empowerment is about developing and using all of the resources that each individual has to offer. This is an essential part of personal congruence.

7. Creating Shared Values

Congruence of values is essential for most people. To align one's own values with those of the organization is key to motivation and commitment.

Creating shared values is about walking the talk—to do the things we believe in and cherish. It means getting it right.

Chapter 3

Values Paradigms

3.1 Values Change

People are often skeptical of the part about changing others' values. Can you change people's values after all? Can you do it as part of a management process? Or should you just try to find values in people that are already there?

It is possible to change values and beliefs. In this chapter we will take a closer look at that.

Recently we had a discussion with a human resource manager from a larger company who was preparing a company-wide management program. In addition, he wanted us to implement a shared values process.

He told us that all of these "soft" expressions of alignment, relationships, teams and congruence were not really management language at their company. They were in it for profit, performance, planning and control. The most prominent approach was, "What's in it for me?"

"Shared values" were something management had heard of at a

seminar. While he was happy to implement it, he feared it would be just a new campaign—a new concept of controlling people by feeding them what they presumably want.

How could this be addressed? In order to make strategic management work, it must involve managing the organizational culture as well. How is this done?

To provide you with that answer, we have to establish a model for interpreting and classifying values paradigms.

3.2 Clare V. Graves

The model that we are going to present here is based on the work of Clare V. Graves, who wrote an article with the odd title, "The Emergent Double Helix Model of Mature Adult Bio-Psychological Behavior." That's not a very friendly name for an article, and not very easy reading, either!

Another source must also be mentioned before we proceed. Don Edward Beck and Christopher C. Cowan wrote a book called, *Spiral Dynamics: Mastering Values, Leadership, and Change* (which is excellent material, yet not very easy reading).

We also want to give credit to Karsten Kock, a Danish Neurolinguistic-Programming (NLP) trainer and friend who has enlightened us on the subject and written some interesting course material.

These ideas take some concentration initially, but the applications are worthwhile. We will share them with you in light of the ideas of congruence and alignment.

We are able to cope with circumstances according to different paradigms. We use the paradigm appropriate for the situation. So, handling different situations means adopting different values paradigms.

The basic ideas can be explained by the following example.

Some time ago a Peruvian lawyer from New York named Evelyn was our guest in Denmark. In our country, a guest from abroad is a guest of honor. So when dinner was served, it was to our surprise that she began to serve everyone at the table.

Curious, we asked what caused her to do this. She explained that in Peru it was traditional that the youngest girl in the family served the others. She assumed that it was the same way in Denmark. By serving us, she acknowledged our hospitality by acting as part of the family.

She added that in Peru she would never speak to the eldest in the family until she had assured herself (by checking with her older sisters) that they would appreciate what she was going to say.

– Finn

People and organizations adopt values paradigms to help them handle the relationship to their surroundings.

The point here is that we use different values paradigms to approach life. As a lawyer in New York, you can imagine that Evelyn had to take on very different roles during the business day. In Peru, she operated under the accepted values of the family.

Knowing this and being able to identify different values paradigms may have a tremendous impact on your ability to diagnose and implement change. It is valuable to identify potential cultural problems in mergers and acquisitions.

We will return to the applications when you have learned the characteristics of the different values paradigms.

3.3 Tools for Diagnosis

Before we go on, you might want to complete an assessment that will give you clues about your own use of different values paradigms. Complete this assessment prior to reading more about the belief sets. That will allow you to do it without any prejudice. After reading through the descriptions, the scoring on pages 108-109 will give you the opportunity to estimate how much you are operating daily in the different values paradigms.

Put an "x" in Column 1 for all of the statements with which you agree. Do nothing with Column 2 before Section 3.

1	2	TEST YOUR GRAVES PREFERENCES
1	2	**Before you read further, put an "x" in Column 1 for all of the statements that you believe to be mostly true.**
	1	There are some things that are right and some things that are wrong.
		Right or wrong is only relevant if I know the context.
		I normally do what feels right for me here and now.
		I feel things are right if everyone agrees to them.
		It feels right when I see myself as a part of a larger meaningful community.
		I think it is right to have a natural respect for the leadership.
	7	The right result is often more important than the way it is achieved.
		Consideration of what is right or wrong is a luxury I can't always allow myself.
		In the long run I will be rewarded for the things I do.
		Most of the time it is possible to create win/win solutions.
		I feel it is important that others show me respect.
		If cooperation works, it isn't so important to get a personal reward.
		It is almost a reward in itself to experience increasing globalization.
	6	It is rewarding in itself to have the security of belonging to a social group.
		I will be rewarded if I am good at giving others what they need.
		It is rewarding in itself that I can manage in life.
		Sometimes fear of punishment will make people do the right thing.

TEST YOUR GRAVES PREFERENCES		
1	**2**	**Before you go on, put an "x" in Column 1 for all of the statements that you believe to be mostly true.**
		I think personal freedom will produce the most acceptable behavior.
		People often have to be forced to maintain certain conduct.
	4	The proper behavior can normally be agreed on by consensus.
		My conduct is determined by my awareness of my purpose in life.
		If I want to feel safe, I have to follow the instructions of management.
		I do what I'm paid to do.
		I do what is necessary to survive.
		I think I am in the place in life that is right for me.
		Everyone basically has the resources necessary to create their own lives.
		I take what I can get in life.
		I grow in life mostly based on my relationships with others.
		I grow in life through an understanding of the greater context of which I am a part.
		I will eventually get respect and status from the wisdom I acquire in my life
		I create my own destiny.
		Life is a jungle and I have to fight for my existence.
		I fight for what is right and fight against what is wrong.
		I fight to understand the deeper connections of things.
		I fight to satisfy my needs.
		I fight to keep good relationships with others.
	5	I fight for the survival of the globe.
		I fight for the social group to which I belong.
		I fight to get my share of all that this world can offer.
		I fight for my own existence.
		Decisions should be made by those who have the authority to do so.
		Many have the ability to make their own decisions.
		The strongest in a group should make the decisions.
		Decisions are a common responsibility in any group.
		Decisions should be made by leaders who are born to do so.

1	2	TEST YOUR GRAVES PREFERENCES
		Before you go on, put an "x" in Column 1 for all of the statements that you believe to be mostly true.
		Those with the most insight in life should make the decisions.
		Eventually, those who have been able to outdo the others make decisions.
		I decide for myself.
	1	People must be held accountable for what they do.
		Opportunity to learn is more important than finding who is responsible.
		The best way to keep people accountable is by immediate consequences.
		Responsibility is not that important if harmony can be achieved.
		There is meaning in the responsibilities I undertake in life.
		I take responsibility that the leaders ask to me take.
		I take responsibility for myself and live with the consequences.
		All in all I only take responsibility for myself.
		Eventually I will get what I deserve.
	2	There is no such thing as a guaranteed result from anything I do.
		If I do not get it now I might never get it.
		Eventually I will get more back from the community than I invest in it.
		We will eventually learn to coexist on earth.
		It's not so important what I get, as long as I belong somewhere.
		I will get what I create for myself.
		I will hardly get more than the right to live an acceptable life.
		An organization that values regulations and procedures gets the best results.
		An organization that values creating understanding of the whole gets the best results.
	3	An organization that values its leaders who have the power to make it happen get the best results.
		An organization that values mutually supportive relationships gets the best results.
		An organization that values networking gets the best results.
		An organization that values traditions and rituals gets the best results.

1	2	TEST YOUR GRAVES PREFERENCES
1	**2**	**Before you go on, put an "x" in Column 1 for all of the statements that you believe to be mostly true.**
		An organization that values objectives and planning gets the best results.
		An organization that values creating a fighting spirit gets the best results.
		Most of my friends share the same values I do.
		I am fascinated by the variations of values among my friends.
		I have lots of friends but few very close ones.
		I consider my friends my companions in life.
	5	My friends and I are part of a global network.
		My friends are the group to which I belong.
		Most of my friends are also my colleagues.
		Actually there isn't anyone you can trust in depth.
		There are things about what is wrong and right that are important to learn early in life.
		I learn best on my own terms.
		I learn by the immediate results I get from what I do.
		I learn by interacting with others in groups.
		I learn by meditation and intuition.
		I learn by example and by modeling.
		I think a little competition improves learning.
		I learn from the "school of hard knocks."
		I prefer to spend my vacations in civilized places.
		Traveling means learning about new things
		When I travel I let my impulses decide the direction.
		Vacation means meeting a lot of new people and making new friends
		When I travel, I feel like a citizen of the world.
	6	Traveling is nice, but only to places that are safe to visit.
		On vacations I look for possibilities to make new interesting business connections.
		In my experience, it can be dangerous to be in unknown surroundings.
		I address colleagues with due respect for their position in the organization.
		I seek colleagues with whom I can discuss subjects of interest.

1	2	TEST YOUR GRAVES PREFERENCES
1	**2**	**Before you go on, put an "x" in Column 1 for all of the statements that you believe to be mostly true.**
		When working with others, I keep a focus on being in control of things.
		I normally seek job assignments in the organization that focus on teamwork.
		I like assignments that build cooperation across borders.
		I like to solve problems that are of importance to everyone in the group.
		I am constantly mindful of my personal career.
		I solve what is important for here and now.
		I prioritize fulfilling my place in the organization.
		I prioritize understanding the culture of the organization.
		I prioritize looking for people in the organization who can challenge me.
		I prioritize looking for people with whom I can create working relationships.
		I prioritize seeking understanding of my organization's place in society.
		I prioritize analyzing what competitors my organization is up against.
		I prioritize looking for my options in the organization.
	8	I prioritize getting butter on my bread every day.

3.4 The Different Values Paradigms

Later on you will determine your assessment score. We will now return to the description of each of the paradigms, then explain how to use them for understanding and planning change.

Before they are described in detail, here are a few introductory comments. First, the belief systems are presented in a sequence. However, this does not indicate ranking. **The judgment you can make about values and belief systems is not one as better than another, but rather, what kind of performance will it lead to in a particular environment or context?** It is the interaction of beliefs with the environment that determines the effectiveness.

72

CLARE V. GRAVES
THE DYNAMICS OF VALUES

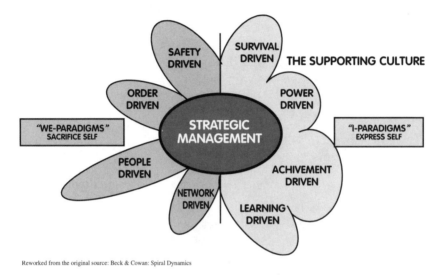

Reworked from the original source: Beck & Cowan: Spiral Dynamics

Second, notice in the model that there are paradigms drawn to the right and paradigms drawn to the left. The difference is because the value systems are in two "families." **The paradigms on the right prioritize individual concerns. The paradigms on the left apply to collective or group thinking.**

Third, every time we describe a values system you will probably reference it to your own values. This is an excellent approach. But don't fall into the trap of "This **is** me" / "This **is not** me. " **The model is not for putting *people* into boxes. The purpose is to examine *belief systems* in order to recognize them, discuss them, diagnose them, and learn about the ways they transform.**

You will probably find that you adopt many of the values paradigms depending on the context. The way to relate it to your own values is: "Those are the values I expose in this or that situation," and, "I rarely do that," or "I often do that."

Fourth, it is important to note that the belief systems are **structure** oriented, not **content** oriented. Each of them can be used or misused. We will provide examples of this for each one as we go along.

For each paradigm, we describe a logical level of change both for individuals exposing those kind of values and for organizations in which those kinds of values dominate. We start each of the descriptions with a diagram to illustrate it.

3.4.1 The Survival Paradigm

The first paradigm is the survival paradigm. This value paradigm works when something important, like a job or our very existence, is at stake.

We have tried to illustrate that in the figure below. Look at the logical levels of change. The **identity** is that of being alone in a dangerous world. The **value** most highly ranked is survival. **Beliefs** accompanying that are mistrust and fighting for one's own share. The valued **skill** is the ability to react.

SURVIVAL DRIVEN
ALONE

	INDIVIDUAL	ORGANIZATIONAL
IDENTITY	AN ANIMAL	A GROUP OF INDIVIDUALS
VALUES	SURVIVE	SURVIVE INDIVIDUALLY
QUALIFICATIONS	REACT	HUNT
BEHAVIOR	FIGHT & PROTECT	FIGHT FOR EXISTENCE
ENVIRONMENT	NO MAN'S LAND	AN UNSTRUCTURED WORLD

Possible **behaviors** are self-defense actions and conflicts over resources. The **environment** seems chaotic and unstructured. It is hostile to existence.

Few people expose these values. Examples might include people on narcotics, psychotic people, or people put into extreme conditions (such as ending up in the jungle after a plane crash). Another example would be very small children just screaming for food and care.

On a particular Friday in the spring of 1998 it was announced in Denmark that there would be a general strike the coming Monday. A lot of people shifted their values to the survival system in minutes and stormed into shops for food, gas and other necessities.

Negotiating with people who carry these values is almost impossible, as they only have a limited consciousness of themselves. These people do not really **organize.** We cannot really find any society organized around these values.

What we can find, though, are organizations temporarily regressing to survival-driven behavior. If organizations announce layoffs without indicating who is next in line, everyone tries to save his or her own skin. Normal cooperation disintegrates.

Managing means, if anything here, caring for the individual. The **learning** style is by reaction and mostly based on sensing. No contextual learning can take place.

The clash of different values systems makes for excellent movies. Imagine the standard film with a group of survivors from an accident. The latent conflict between working as a team (this is Graves' "people" paradigm—we will come to that) and the fight for individual survival creates the scene for drama.

3.4.2 The Safety Paradigm

When people find that the fight for survival is too lonely and hard, they organize in tribe-like organizations. This is the first "sacrifice self" system, where the collective values take priority over the individual.

75

SAFETY DRIVEN
TRIBAL

	INDIVIDUAL	ORGANIZATIONAL
IDENTITY	A MEMBER	A TRIBE
VALUES	SEEK SAFETY	BE TOGETHER AND SAFE
QUALIFICATIONS	ADAPT	CREATE RITUALS - DEFEND OURSELVES
BEHAVIOR	DELIVER SERVICE	PROTECT OURSELVES
ENVIRONMENT	THE TRIBE	A DANGEROUS WORLD

The **identity** is that of a clan or tribe member who has banded together with others for safety. The identity is closely connected to a sense of "belonging." Typical tribal **values** are safety and tradition. Tribal members **believe** that the leader should be the one to make decisions, and they believe they will be rewarded for loyalty because of the respect they show the leader.

The members **learn** to be able to fulfill the needs of the leader and the group.

Possible **behaviors** include significant peer pressure to remain loyal to the group. The members adhere to rituals. Questioning current practices is discouraged. The members might even dress according to tribal norms to strengthen the sense of belonging.

Tribal leaders could be a chieftain, a shaman, the elders, a CEO, or a Mafia boss. Tribal **organizations** exist in many families and in small societies as well.

Be careful here; feelings about Mafia bosses might not be exactly the same as the feelings for chieftains. So the *content* is extremely different, but the *structure* is the same. Graves' classifications are entirely descriptive of structures, not content.

This paradigm works best when an effective leader has the best interests of the followers at heart. This belief system may be suited to cope with situations where the leader has special abilities, insight or experience that group members do not yet possess.

From an organizational point of view, this is interesting because you often find this type of organization. If you want to **negotiate** with a tribal organization, you have to negotiate with the chief. Before you negotiate, you would probably try to obtain as much information as possible about the chief's opinions from other members in order to please him or her.

Decisions are made entirely by the leader based on personal needs and traditions.

This is also something we have seen in popular movies. The hero and the heroine are stranded among natives on an island. They violate the honor they should show to the tribal chief, thereby bringing themselves into extreme danger of becoming the next meal!

Managers in this paradigm believe in nepotism. They are primarily there to satisfy themselves. They expect obedience according to tradition and rituals. They expect everyone to sacrifice themselves for the tribe.

Learning in these surroundings takes place in a particular way. People learn by example, by repeating the leader's behavior or by sequential step-by-step type of learning. This is typically supported by rituals and routines. Many rituals support long-term learning and loyalty to the tribe. Nothing is learned that is not a part of the approved wisdom of the tribe. You might recognize this from Jean M. Auel's, "The Clan of The Cave Bear" if you are familiar with it.

3.4.3 The Power Paradigm

Some individuals rely on their own power to manage. The feeling of **identity** is closely related to the sense of power they have.

POWER DRIVEN
EMPIRE

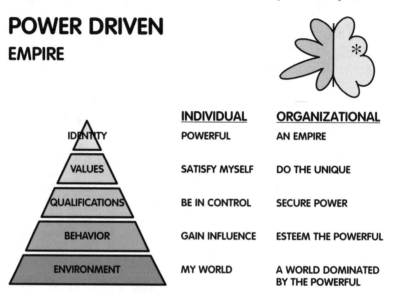

	INDIVIDUAL	ORGANIZATIONAL
IDENTITY	POWERFUL	AN EMPIRE
VALUES	SATISFY MYSELF	DO THE UNIQUE
QUALIFICATIONS	BE IN CONTROL	SECURE POWER
BEHAVIOR	GAIN INFLUENCE	ESTEEM THE POWERFUL
ENVIRONMENT	MY WORLD	A WORLD DOMINATED BY THE POWERFUL

Typically, power-driven **values** include the right to immediate self-satisfaction. The **beliefs** are that others must be dominated, that immediate results are what counts, and that things must be controlled. According to this, "time" and "waiting" are almost non-existent.

Typical beliefs would also include that power earns the right to have more than others of everything—status, money and all kinds of material assets. Accordingly, the paradigm does not recognize "guilt." Any kind of satisfaction is well deserved despite the means that were used to obtain it. As a result, feedback is of no interest.

The **skill** that is perfected here is the ability to control others.

In this paradigm, **organizations** are typically power based. The prized members are the most powerful or the most excellent in their profession.

We see this type of system often in the media. It appears in society as criminal activity on the streets and in the Wild West. In the movies we see many roles that represent "power," such as Jack Nicholson in *One Flew Over the Cuckoo's Nest*. On the individual level we might include many adolescents(!).

If you want to **negotiate** with these people, think twice. This paradigm does not have any sense of time. Your opponent would say "yes" to your suggestions only because it seems to make you happy just now. To live with the later consequence is not a consideration. This is precisely why resocializing criminals by talking with them has a limited effect.

To negotiate, you have to rely on the very nature of this paradigm: power and satisfaction. To resocialize someone, present him or her with new ways to achieve the same satisfaction.

Negotiating in business is from your power base. **Decisions** are entirely made by the tough minded based on what feels good now. Short term results are what counts.

Managers are recruited, selected, and promoted for their individual drive, initiative, and ability to quickly deliver. They believe that others have to be dominated to keep them from following their immediate lust. Nobody can really be trusted and everybody can be bought.

The **learning** style is based on satisfaction and power. An example is the parent who pays his child for every "A." Direct action is a key factor for learning. The concern is, "What's in it for me now?"

Emphasis is placed on action and competition instead of procedures. No guilt is involved, so mutual respect is not valued.

3.4.4 The Order Paradigm

The order driven paradigm views the world as predictable and orderly. Things are stable and one can count on them. There is justice. There are reasons for what you see around you, even if you don't always know the reasons. **Identity** is closely related to being part of a civilized society.

ORDER DRIVEN
HIERARCHY

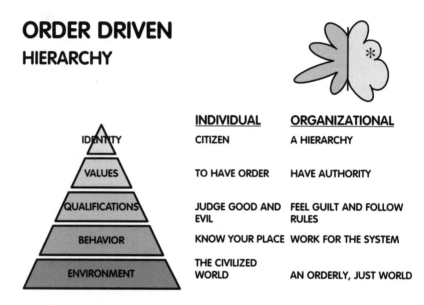

	INDIVIDUAL	ORGANIZATIONAL
IDENTITY	CITIZEN	A HIERARCHY
VALUES	TO HAVE ORDER	HAVE AUTHORITY
QUALIFICATIONS	JUDGE GOOD AND EVIL	FEEL GUILT AND FOLLOW RULES
BEHAVIOR	KNOW YOUR PLACE	WORK FOR THE SYSTEM
ENVIRONMENT	THE CIVILIZED WORLD	AN ORDERLY, JUST WORLD

The **values** exposed would be that people must wait for rewards because they will come as a result of sustained performance of acceptable behavior. The **beliefs** are that justice exists and that rules and regulations are necessary to keep things under control. Decisions should be made by those who have authority and made according to the rules.

The **skills** to be perfected are to play by the rules and distinguish right from wrong.

The **behavior** is according to rules and procedures that apply to the position you have. There are punishments for those who don't stay in their place. There are many forms of "permission slips" to be signed by those with the proper authority. (Examples: Travel reimbursement forms, time cards, etc.)

Excellent behavior is having a strong sense for preserving order, organization and justice. Repulsive behavior would be low tolerance for those who think differently. They can be cruel—crushing "wrong thinking" people if they do not comply with the rules and regulations. The nurse in *One Flew Over the Cuckoo's Nest* is an example.

In this paradigm, time and guilt are dominant factors. To have the correct behavior might not be rewarded right away. Emphasis is on delayed gratification. You will be rewarded with a gold watch after 25 years of loyal service or even heaven after life itself.

Many organizations are built on these values. Government institutions are an example. Many private enterprises also work like this. In this paradigm, people **organize** in traditional hierarchies. This type of organization is represented everywhere. Everybody has their proper place and their job description. This is useful if the environment is not experiencing rapid change. But job descriptions have a tendency to freeze things like many tools have in the "order" paradigm. Many management tools derive from this paradigm, even though this paradigm is not best-suited for coping with a changing environment.

The "order" paradigm is therefore currently the one most organizations attempt to leave, but don't know how. Many organizations dominated by this paradigm may be doomed as change hits the organization. The "order" paradigm of controlling by authority is the very one that you have to rethink and partly leave if you want to handle reality and transform to an adaptive, creative organization for the future.

In movies, we like to see conflicts of the "order" system with the "power" system. For instance, the noble but naive policeman who comes into conflict with his "power" colleagues who beat up the suspects before they bring them in. Or the aging former "power"—cowboy who has settled in on his farm (the "order" paradigm) and returns to the big city to save it from the "power" villains that are terrorizing it.

To **negotiate** with these people you have to refer to right or wrong. Emphasize doing it the right way and getting the just and right results. You have to address the right person. Identify the person that is allowed by the system to make the decision. **Decisions** are based on authority and rules.

Managers are the ones with the authority that the system gives them. They think of the organization as a machine. People can be put into positions and work accordingly. Responsibility will be assigned to explain every little failure. This is a belief that is nurtured in the press every day. Every time something goes wrong, journalists inevitably find a politician who is willing to state publicly that responsibility in this matter has been placed on someone's shoulders.

Responsibility for failures from experimentation is just about the most damaging belief system you may adopt if you want to promote learning. Learning itself implies trial and error. That's why a learning organization is almost impossible to implement in an "order" paradigm.

The **learning** style of the "order" paradigm is by authority and procedure. Reward and punishment are part of the incentives that are used for expressing the ability to distinguish right from wrong. Certificates on the wall would be the way to prove that you passed.

Amazingly, many of us have been unsuspecting "victims" of this type of learning. Nevertheless, we find it the way to go when dealing with our children.

In many families we hear children say, "I'll never be like that!" but the pattern continues. We tend to act according to the role models we know.

3.4.5 The Achievement Paradigm

The achievement paradigm represents very typical business values. The identity is one of being in charge of one's own life—being a winner.

ACHIEVEMENT DRIVEN
"SUCCESS"

	INDIVIDUAL	ORGANIZATIONAL
IDENTITY	A WINNER	A "SUCCESSFUL" BUSINESS
VALUES	HAVE SUCCESS	IMPROVE AND MAKE MONEY
QUALIFICATIONS	ORGANIZE	PLAN AND REACH OUR GOALS
BEHAVIOR	BUILD	WORK FOR OURSELVES
ENVIRONMENT	A COMPETITIVE WORLD	A COMPETITIVE MARKET

Typical **values** would be attaining success as the consequence of setting goals, planning and risk-taking. In this paradigm, popularity and prestige are also present together with the drive for conquering the world. The basic question is, "What's in it for me?"

The dominant **beliefs** would be that goals can be set, all work can be organized and planned. There are unlimited possibilities, not the least of which are due to technology. Belief in science is unlimited. Everything is possible if we invest the money needed and get the political support. In the extreme, these people can even cut down rain forests for profit with the belief that someone will replenish it again using the proper technology.

The **qualifications** you would want to perfect are strategic thinking and planning skills.

This is the thinking that created the Industrial Revolution and the traditional American Businessman. The **behavior** here is entrepreneurial. The remarkable difference from the "power" paradigm is the sense of time. Here immediate gratification is not the only issue. Strategic planning for even greater goals is more relevant.

The achievement-driven **organization** is not very far from the "order" paradigm. We have by no means left the concept of authority and hierarchy. We have revised it a little, though, by allowing more flexible project-oriented features to handle different tasks. Right or wrong is not as much in focus as are results and achievement.

This is also very commonly found in society. Excellent examples are constructive and entrepreneurial businesspersons at their best. Repulsive would be the swindlers and small time criminals that go bankrupt to save their own money at the expense of their creditors.

To **negotiate** in this paradigm you have to appeal to "what's in it for me." Motivators are profit, better paying jobs, winning, and being on top of things. **Decisions** are based almost exclusively on bottom-line results.

Managers believe in competition. You will find individual sales performance figures on the walls and incentives for every desired behavior. There are tools for every behavior you want to encourage —all of them based on people's desire for material achievements and status.

A typical management scheme would be "performance management." This is a fine example of trying to link business goals to individual performance. The weakness of the usual approach, we know now, is that this does not necessarily create congruence and alignment of values, but only of behavior.

The **learning** style here is predominantly practical. Many managers at courses sit down with no more than half an hour with the theoretical framework before they ask for the tools to take home. Investing their time in insight is rare. But amazingly enough, we experience that the most shrewd and best performing "achievement" business leaders do take advantage of theoretical insight that gives them a boost for their negotiations.

Learning also would be competitive. This is something that keynote speakers often take advantage of by giving away gadgets and books to clever listeners. Individuals are rewarded for answering questions.

One of the problems with the "achievement" paradigm is the disregard for feelings and other non-measurable factors. In the movies we see it when the children of hard-hearted "achievement" business fathers become "weak" and overcome with emotion. It drives home the fact that this can be an imbalanced approach with too much emphasis on profit and too little caring.

3.4.6 The People Paradigm

The people paradigm represents the value of relationships. The **identity** or self-concept is that of a peer among equals. Typical **values** here are to build relationships, act in consensus and take care of everyone's needs in the process of doing things.

The way to achieve things becomes as important as the result. The **belief** is that people buy into a common goal more easily when they are involved in the process.

Skills you would want to perfect are communication, networking and functioning as a team player.

PEOPLE DRIVEN
TEAMS

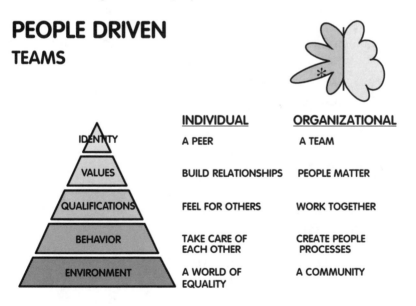

	INDIVIDUAL	ORGANIZATIONAL
IDENTITY	A PEER	A TEAM
VALUES	BUILD RELATIONSHIPS	PEOPLE MATTER
QUALIFICATIONS	FEEL FOR OTHERS	WORK TOGETHER
BEHAVIOR	TAKE CARE OF EACH OTHER	CREATE PEOPLE PROCESSES
ENVIRONMENT	A WORLD OF EQUALITY	A COMMUNITY

Behavior would typically be directed at taking care of others' needs and ensuring that rights were respected. Excellent behavior is creating warm productive relationships with others along with social responsibility. More repulsive behavior might be "wishy-washy inefficiency" and no sense of the need for creating results.

The way people want to **organize** here is in teams, as teams lend themselves to methods that take care of internal relationships and acknowledge everyone's unique contribution. They have low respect for authority.

To **negotiate** with these people you have to communicate and establish relationships. You have to respect that the process of agreeing is as important as the result itself. **Decisions** are based on consensus.

Managers believe in acceptance, sharing and relationships. Emotions are something that managers have to address. People work harder if they participate and engage in the decision-making process.

Typical management schools of thought include "Quality Circles," "Conflict Management Programs" and "Emotional Intelligence."

The **learning** style here is predominantly collective and based on interaction between the learners. The leader becomes a facilitator that initiates the processes that lead to learning. Competition is out of the question.

The "people" paradigm is becoming increasingly valuable in today's environment. Human capital is being recognized as a key organizational asset.

3.4.7 The Learning Paradigm

The "learning" paradigm is the paradigm of understanding processes. Typical **identity** here is closely linked to that of a learner in a system.

In this paradigm **values** are on systemic thinking, including how to learn and coexist in a complex world. From this perspective, acceptance of others and differences are fascinating subjects. "Learning" values include finding win/win situations for everyone —freedom for oneself but not abusing anyone to have it.

The predominant belief is that life has endless depths of insight worth pursuing. Truth and reality are relative to an individual's perception.

LEARNING DRIVEN
PROCESS THINKING

	INDIVIDUAL	ORGANIZATIONAL
IDENTITY	SYSTEMS ANALYST	LEARNING
VALUES	WIN/WIN SOLUTIONS	ACCEPT OTHERS
QUALIFICATIONS	CREATE STRUCTURE	SEE THROUGH SYSTEMS
BEHAVIOR	WORK WITHOUT CONSULTANCY	WORK TO CREATE UNDERSTANDING
ENVIRONMENT	A DATA-RICH WORLD	A SYSTEMATIC NETWORK ECONOMY

Typical **behavior** is learning oriented—either learning yourself or working as a consultant, coach, trainer or teacher. Examples include researchers, Sherlock Holmes, analysts and the best of journalism. Information is used to improve and learn. Repulsive behavior might be those who gather endless streams of information, but do not put anything into perspective.

Negotiating in this paradigm means to make sense in the broader perspective. Personal freedom and an appreciation of tolerance and flexibility will motivate individuals. Decisions are based on principles and knowledge. Here no one acknowledges authoritarian rules and no one is compliant with dogmatic thinking or a singular "truth."

The paradigm **organizes** according to circumstances—always looking for the best possible approach for that particular context.

The **learning** style in this environment is self-motivated, looking for insight perhaps for no other particular reason than the satisfaction of knowing. Therefore, the leader has to give access to data and knowledge and facilitate identification of new areas for exploration. Competition does not figure in here, as everyone exercises their individual freedom to learn. Rewards are intrinsic.

Few of these people want to be **managers** themselves, but if they do, they manage by tools like free access to information. They motivate by values and learning and not by "carrot and stick." They use differences as a leveraging factor for the company's competitive edge and do not believe in achieving ultimate goals. They create fluid conditions with temporary goals adapting to change.

3.4.8 The Network Paradigm

The "network" paradigm is the paradigm of the global society. The **identity** is that of a member of a closely linked interdependent system.

NETWORK DRIVEN
INTERCONNECTED
- A GLOBAL COMMUNITY

	INDIVIDUAL	ORGANIZATIONAL
IDENTITY	INTERDEPENDENT	LIVING ORGANISM
VALUES	BE GLOBALLY RESPONSIBLE	SECURE THE SURVIVAL OF ALL OF US
QUALIFICATIONS	SEE THE WHOLE CONTEXT	WORK TOGETHER/ MACRO VIEW
BEHAVIOR	STEWARD OF RESOURCES	EMBRACE PARADOX
ENVIRONMENT	BORDERLESS	A UNIFIED FORCE

This paradigm considers society as an integrated village. Human-made boundaries become less relevant. Values are placed on worthy purposes like eliminating hunger, war and poverty, and on creating a meaningful life in harmony with nature. "Live simply so that others may simply live" is a motto.

Skills to be achieved would be ability to preserve and restore global resources and gain insight into the way ecological systems work.

Typical **behavior** would be disregarding artificial borders, embracing paradox, and seeking invention of environmentally-friendly technology.

Excellent behavior would be environmentally conscious people and repulsive behavior would be people who use knowledge about global resources to exploit those resources in a careless way.

Typically this is **organized** in a network. Emphasis is on connectedness. The way the internet functions certainly fits in this paradigm.

Organizations must take responsibility for the impact of their actions. This paradigm is the one that is emerging more clearly in recent years.

In fiction, Jules Verne, and as a scientist, John Naisbit, might be in this paradigm. Kevin Kelly's book, *Out of Control*, examines this view.

Managing here includes what is spiritual and purposeful. People are a part of one another—one dynamic living organism. People are motivated by an overall quality of life for all.

Negotiating must include an appeal to the "macro view." There is a need to see everything at once before determining a course of action. It can embrace paradox. Decisions are based on individual freedoms as well as the strengthening of the community.

Learning is holistic. It includes information as well as our feelngs about it. It encompasses intuition. Both conscious and subconscious elements of our mind are seen as valid. It acknowledges spirituality; that there is more than we can ever truly know and understand.

3.4.9 The Organizational Principles

Let's presume that each of the paradigms is a set of values that can be used to cope with the outside world. They are descriptive for individuals but equally descriptive for organizations. Groups tend to organize according to their values set. These are the eight organizational cultures most often found.

ORGANIZATIONAL PRINCIPLES

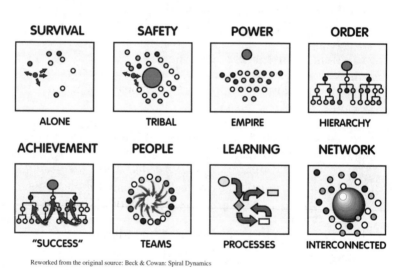

Reworked from the original source: Beck & Cowan: Spiral Dynamics

3.4.10 Metaphoric Language

Let's look more closely at how to recognize the culture.

One way we reveal mental assumptions is by the words and metaphors we use. If you listen carefully to the language used in an organization, you get additional clues as to which culture you are dealing with.

Words like success, planning, invention, technology, and goal-setting indicate the "achievement" paradigm.

Expressions of justice, right, wrong, responsibility, authority, keeping one's place—the "order" paradigm apparently.

Words like loyalty, family, tradition, belonging, respect, security are a part of the "safety" clan paradigm.

Think of an organization that describes the market as "a war out there." What could you imagine their values paradigm to be?

They would be **warriors**—the competition **enemies.** Thinking of win/win would be almost impossible. Victory is the end goal, which means defeat for others. Your workplace would be like your home base—the fortress. Entrance would be restricted. Discipline would be required. Loyalty would be mandatory. Society would be the infrastructure to provide for the war.

Most likely we are in the "safety" paradigm.

What about an organization that uses phrases like "We are players in the marketplace"?

They would be **players**—competitive **players,** too. Stakes would be placed in order to gain a profit. What's in it for us? Alliances would be possible if they produced results. The office would be like a chess board; people are welcome to play the game and be on our side. Creativity as well as discipline would be rewarded.

Most likely we are in the "achievement" paradigm.

> *People and organizations often reveal their values paradigms in the language and the metaphors they use.*

3.4.11 Non-productive Collective Assumptions

Sometimes when you try to recognize a particular culture, stereotypes and non-productive assumptions appear in the process. They might also give you the clue to the dominant culture.

Look at the assumptions below. They can have the same counterproductive effect on the culture as some beliefs have on individuals.

No.	Paradigm	Assumption
2	The tribe – "safety"	✔ If you say your honest opinion, you get fired. ✔ You must propose the solution in the way you think your boss will accept it. ✔ We are not here to think.
3	The dictatorship – "power"	✔ People cheat if they can. ✔ We cannot plan and control as things might change tomorrow. ✔ Managers cling to & deserve power.
4	The hierarchy – "order"	✔ What is not allowed is not possible. ✔ When a decision is made it cannot be changed. ✔ We have not seen the last system of control yet. ✔ More resources mean better service. ✔ It's the shop stewards who run the show here (not the "people" paradigm – unions are typically "right or wrong" organizations) ✔ Managers should know everything.
5	The business – "achievement"	✔ People only do what they are rewarded for. ✔ We have so many balls in the air— none of them is ever going to land. ✔ We have a job to take care of. ✔ We always invest in new technology to get ahead. ✔ Those of us on the shop floor are going to be changed, but not management. ✔ It's not so bad if someone else fails. ✔ They do not do a full day's work in public offices. ✔ There are no problems we cannot solve. ✔ Managers should always be busy.

No.	Paradigm	Assumption
6	The team – "people"	✔ If you have shared information with one, you have probably shared it with everyone. ✔ You cannot back out without being marked as negative. ✔ We hold meetings just for the sake of the meetings. ✔ We are open and honest, but not always. ✔ We lack communication across the organization.
7	The Learning Organization – "systemic"	✔ We do not allocate the resources and the time needed for the jobs. ✔ Here we cherish freedom of choice above all else. ✔ You make your own limits. ✔ People are free to choose for themselves.
8	The network – "Global"	✔ If it's done to me, it's done to all of us. ✔ As the internet evolves, the world will be run by technogeeks. ✔ The world leaders are more centered on power than on doing what's needed to save the planet.

Naturally, there are positive assumptions as well. The nicest one we have heard is:

"If you are a bird, then fly!"

This covers the collective assumption that people should be able to use all of their resources. (It belongs to the "learning" paradigm.)

3.5 Planning for Change

We now turn to some of the real benefits of being able to diagnose dominant belief systems in organizations or in smaller groups of managers or employees.

If an organization wants to implement certain behavioral patterns —like support for strategic plans, innovation, or particular business results—the analysis of dominant paradigms allows you to see what is needed to create the particular culture that will support your goals.

Let's look at some examples where knowledge of these paradigms creates instant understanding.

3.5.1 The Learning Organization

As previously mentioned, learning organizations are based on Graves' "learning" values. Many organizations have grasped the idea that putting a priority on knowledge management will improve performance and behavior.

It sounds so credible: "We are a learning organization."

One of the features of a learning organization is that learning is accelerated in teams. Many interpret this to mean teams are mandatory for a learning organization. They are not. Learning can be accelerated in a multitude of other ways. Nevertheless, teams are the predominant tool in most learning organizations.

But what happens? Teams are based on the participants showing Graves' "people" values. However, most managers from private enterprises with "achievement" values or from the public sector with "order" values are not particularly in alignment with "people" values.

So they treat teams like tools ("achievement") or hierarchical instruments ("order") and get a lot of disappointed employees who really commit themselves to "people" values—believing that they were finally going to be listened to and respected.

Add to this that learning is inherently connected with honest feedback and a risk of failure. These are not standard values in "power"/"order"/"achievement" organizations. So, no learning organization will emerge as long as the organizational values do not include "people"/"learning" values.

Last, one more way to view the learning organization is to go with Peter Senge and look at the whole thing from a systems perspective —the "learning" paradigm. In Senge's book, *The Fifth Discipline*, systems understanding is at the heart of the learning/process perspective of organizations.

> *Creating a learning organization means to adopt some "people"/"learning" values—or forget it.*

3.5.2 Management Schools

There are many ways to teach management. In this context some important issues become more apparent.

CLASSICAL MANAGEMENT IN A NON-ADAPTIVE CULTURE

Teaching strategic management—long term planning, goal setting, policies, project management and action plans—are a subset of the "order" and "achievement" management values. Many business schools teach these skills as the backbone of their belief system. Other disciplines like the learning organization or team-based management are just tools for controlling behavior in a new sophisticated way. They never change the basic values of "order" and "achievement" management.

We have tried to illustrate this in the figure on the previous page. The predominant cultural beliefs are signified by making the particular "wings" of the culture oversized.

It is a difficult task to convince "achievement"-oriented people to invest in their employees. Their view is mechanistic and they like having the direct reason why something should work and what results to expect. An investment in people takes time and is based on probability. It does not give them enough control over the results.

But the mechanistic achievement paradigm does not adequately suffice in an environment that calls for adaptability. "Bio-logical" creativity is needed because complex systems do not lend themselves to a centralized management structure.

STRATEGIC MANAGEMENT IN A HIGHLY SUPPORTING CULTURE

Other management schools, therefore, take a genuine "learning" or "people" perspective of management. One example is the book you are reading at this moment. We don't disregard "achievement," as strategic planning is still the heart of business. The suggestion is to enrich "achievement" values by incorporating "people" and "learning" values as well. This is what will enable you to deal with the current environment most effectively.

The figure on the previous page shows the "wings" of "order" slightly less dominant and the "wings" of "achievement", "people" and "learning" most pronounced.

3.5.3 Crossing Borders & Cultures

Writing this book as a cross-cultural project was also rather intruiging and entertaining. The Danish culture is basically "order" and "people," even sometimes a "network" culture. Danes as a whole do not emphasize individuals. They tend to emphasize justice, equality and caring for others.

Mainstream American business culture, on the other hand, is much more "order" (hierarchies) "power" (heroes) and "achievement" (the business person) driven. Many more are self-employed, and success is a key value.

American culture often rewards individual "heroes" for their achievements. In Denmark, the emphasis is somewhat more group oriented.

This became quite evident when we entered discussion with a potential business partner. The person explained, "Currently, I receive 25% of any client I bring in to the company. How do you handle this?"

We explained, "Oh, we would never consider that. We work together, and all compensation is divided knowing that each of us has something to contribute. I might have a good year this year, but next year it could be you who carries the day."

The Graves model permits us in a simple way to discuss and to relate to basic cultural differences and describe in detail some diversity issues.

It also gives insight into why cross-cultural cooperation can be so beneficial or so burdensome. There are so many more paradigms to handle! There is potential for misunderstanding and conflict as well as much learning and growth.

3.5.4 An Example: Implementing TQM

At one time we were invited to a large organization that had tried to implement Total Quality Management (TQM). The effort did not have the impact they expected.

This was a traditional hierarchical organization. It was founded around the start of the century. There were a few extreme union members trying to apply political pressure through unlawful activities. To some degree, the managers were lower level managers of the classical type. Small clans of certain middle managers formed within the company.

The organizational leaders tried to implement TQM by running a large education program teaching everybody about methods and technologies for maintaining and developing quality and working in teams. Managers had learned the tools, too, and several cross-functional teams worked to improve key business processes.

What do we have here? We have an "order" culture, with managers trying to run the business as a tribe and "power" elements trying to sabotage it.

Adding to this, we have top management trying to form the whole thing into an "achievement" business. They buy the consultants' "systems" perspective and allow for a project to teach all the tools necessary to implement a TQM culture based on "learning" and "people" values.

A CHANGE PROJECT

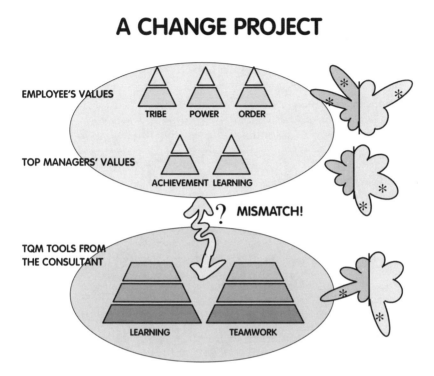

EMPLOYEE'S VALUES

TRIBE   POWER   ORDER

TOP MANAGERS' VALUES

ACHIEVEMENT   LEARNING

?   MISMATCH!

TQM TOOLS FROM
THE CONSULTANT

LEARNING   TEAMWORK

> ***Trying to implement tools that have no support in the
> present value systems of the organization is fruitless.***

No wonder they did not get anywhere. What are the options here?
How could the change be better introduced?

Questions to ask might be, "Is learning quality improvement an
imperative response to market needs, or is it just a trendy idea of
management? Is there any more logical response that would re-
quire less of a values revolution at present?"

Another question to ask is, "What present values would we be able
to introduce in order to build a transition in the culture?" Could it

be based on "order"—being the *right* thing to do? Leading to a *reward in the end?*

At last, we would have to introduce the new values paradigm of TQM. It is an "achievement", "people", and "learning" blend that managers first have to buy into, and employees later on. Getting there is hard work and may involve years of intense effort.

> *Changing qualifications and behavior lead to absolutely nothing if values and identity do not follow.*

3.5.5 An Example from Social Institutions

We have worked for some years with a local county in Denmark and their organization of 70 social institutions. We have conducted a number of projects, but the most important has been training the managers in the principles of learning organizations and values-based management.

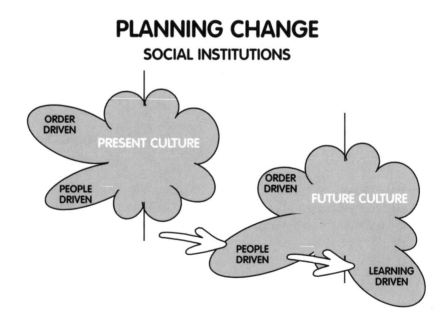

PLANNING CHANGE
SOCIAL INSTITUTIONS

How did we go about it?

To understand this, you have to know that social services are moving toward a philosophy where clients (users) of the system are not "given" influence over their own situation, but are considered to have these rights from the outset. Clients do not only have rights to live their own life in conditions that are the very best for them, they also have the right to be treated as individuals. This is turning things completely upside down from just 15 years ago when institutions tried to make clients adjust to the conditions of the system.

The diagnosis here is an "order" and sometimes "people" culture that wanted to become a workplace with high adaptability. They wanted the ability to discard old dogmatic thinking and create excellent relationships between clients and employees.

We set out to build a genuine "people" culture with a "learning" perspective. They needed to be able to break previous assumptions from the "order" culture. The organization was to be built on teams. The managers were to adopt team-based management and learning organization principles, along with the thinking behind this book as a solid "learning" foothold. We could not completely leave the "order" culture as they were still part of a political system requiring hierarchy.

The figure on the opposite page illustrates the break away from "order" via "people" values to "learning/processes."

In any system you find "achievement" criteria to be met. In a government system this will mainly be bureaucrats and politicians who will demand "achievement" results. In this case, **we achieved a decrease in sick days to half of the previous level and a reduction in staff turnover.** (This is a very physically demanding place to work.) These results by all means met the politicians' bottom line criteria, at the same time meeting the real scope of the program: to create desirable conditions for the clients.

3.5.6 An Example from Private Enterprise

Let's consider the case of an insurance company that has emerged from several mergers and acquisitions, blending at least three different cultures together. It's a successful company, and like many other successful companies it is trying to do better. (A continual pursuit of excellence is what makes the difference between successful companies and those who are not successful.)

Their focus is to create a common culture and prepare for the future. This will entail intensive use of technology, individualized customer service, high accessibility for customers, values-based relationships with customers, and easy access to qualified people.

What we essentially have is a cultural blend of "achievement" (they are talented business people) and "order" (the financial sector being somewhat autocratic and hierarchical) and with occasional aspects of "learning" (a systems perspective of the development in the market and of technology).

What they want is to reinforce management to strengthen "learning" but most of all include the "people" perspectives in management. The inclusion of "people" will allow people to es-

PLANNING CHANGE
PRIVATE ENTERPRISE

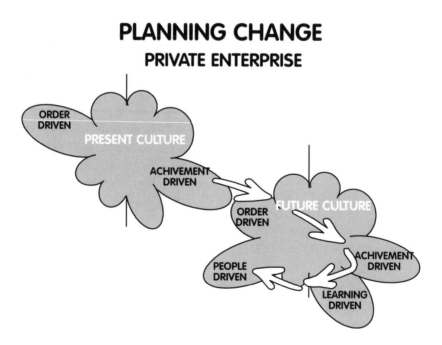

tablish better working relationships, create more cross-functional teamwork and increase understanding of the market and the customers' reactions.

Leaving "order" will permit the organization to move faster and adopt a values-based approach. It will make possible the creation of a strong culture that basically determines behavior via core values and business goals.

They have their own appreciation of this and have already started a process of establishing common business goals as well as common core values.

In this case, the first step to take is from "achievement" to "learning." Moving directly into "people" makes less sense and creates a sense of insecurity.

Notice the movement: "achievement"-"learning"-"people". This is different from the other example "order"-"people"-"learning." Transitions from one paradigm to another cannot be randomly approached. You have to move along the path that creates the most acceptance.

In Beck and Cowan's, *Spiral Dynamics: Mastering Values, Leadership, and Change,* it is mentioned that part of the difficulty in the Korean and Vietnamese wars was the fact that the military still operated in an "order"/"achievement" paradigm. "Operation Desert Storm" represented a new "achievement"/ "people"/ "learning" paradigm of warfare where conditions involved high technology, high mobility and rapid response.

There was a breakdown of hierarchical boundaries through information technology, military experts running the strategic scenarios instead of politicians, dispersed power and authority, and finally rank, power and privilege suppressed for functionality, knowledge and competence. These were modeled congruently by Norman Schwartzkopf himself.

3.5.7 Pressed for Change

We have learned from chapter two that change only occurs when all logical levels change. From this chapter we can now add that this is likely to happen when values and beliefs do not effectively handle the external environment any more.

Sometimes that's not so easy and there are extreme reactions. The picture below illustrates the "panic" reaction of a company where top management just announced that 20% of the workforce must be laid off. Suddenly the survival paradigm appears on the surface.

You have probably met a lot of "power" managers. Their reaction to difficult times is to press full speed ahead. They move about in the organization and create tremendous frustration by starting to do other people's jobs their way—simply because they have lost confidence in the organization.

VALUES UNDER PRESSURE

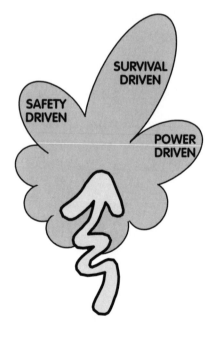

Or you have met "order" managers engaging in personal inquisitions in the organization to get rid of those who think in different ways.

If "achievement" managers find themselves in trouble, they may be susceptible to unethical business methods such as trying to cut dubious deals, resorting to mild blackmail or whatever it takes to get on top again.

Last year a doctor told us about an organizational experiment in his ward about developing patient quality. He received the annual award for the most interesting project in the hospital sector. Then someone asked him about the present status of the project. He answered that management closed down his ward because it didn't comply with the local hospital standards and therefore set a dangerous example for the other wards. "Order" can be cruel.

In the face of stress, "people" managers will probably engage in "holier than thou" or politically correct crusades that will seem like a fall back to "order." Feelings are the way to go—as long as they are the right ones!

Finally, "learning" managers under stress might calculate the probability to win and leave the scene if the odds are too low.

3.5.8 More Caveats on Facilitating Change

Needs are defined by internal and external conditions. Constant flow between paradigms is desirable for organizations that want to survive in the long term.

Facilitating change then must at least in part be based on "learning" or "network" values, because they include respect, understanding and acceptance of all the others.

"Learning" values and tools would therefore be the manager's starting point from where other desired paradigms can be introduced according to organizational needs.

> **To facilitate change you have to create a learning environment that regularly confronts previous beliefs with new ones.**

We had a client last year who made a lot of money, but nevertheless was brought into a dangerous position by the financial crisis in the Far East. That's one of the most dangerous positions to be in because theoretical threats like this are hard to grasp in large, successful organizations. Measures to adapt could be completely misunderstood.

Trying to handle the situation directly could lead to immediate disaster. Clever facilitation means consciously developing the crisis as a scenario until a general acceptance of the need for change can be reached.

> **Creating the crisis scenario can be part of introducing a new paradigm.**

To adopt a new paradigm may be a crisis in one's life. Sometimes improving performance within a paradigm might be more helpful to handle reality. Out of this we might cautiously conclude

> **Sometimes the best solution for change is learning to cope better within the existing paradigm.**

3.6 Tools for Diagnosis Continued

We have now learned that creating change and a culture of commitment depends on an understanding of the values and beliefs that dominate the present culture.

To understand fully, we cannot entirely rely on listening to language use and metaphors. Those are ways to get started; however, additional means of measurement are needed.

An important first question to answer is if the collective culture matches the beliefs of individuals working in it. This is by no means self evident. Look at the illustration below. The corporate culture might show major signs of order and power and the employee's values might be somewhat different—people and network. We have examples of precisely this situation for several clients. This is a culture where teamwork is the desire of employees but the supporting management style, systems and rules do not favor that kind of cooperation.

An analysis such as this of the whole group of employees or of subgroups, sectors or managers might reveal major discrepancies in alignment. Such gaps could prove dangerous to long term survival and must be addressed in an implementation plan.

GAP BETWEEN THE COLLECTIVE CULTURE AND THE PERSONAL VALUES OF INDIVIDUALS WITHIN IT

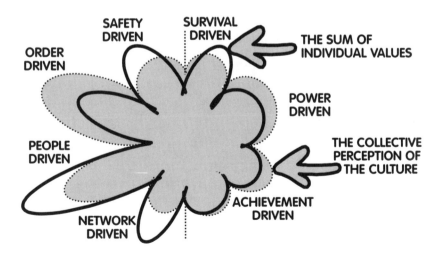

3.6.1 Measuring Progress

When you plan interventions for change, you will want to track shifts in culture accordingly.

Intervention strategies could be management seminars, employee training programs, coaching, implementation of new performance management systems, etc.

Simultaneous measurement of strategic results would then prove if the culture starts to support business goals as intended.

MEASURING PROGRESS

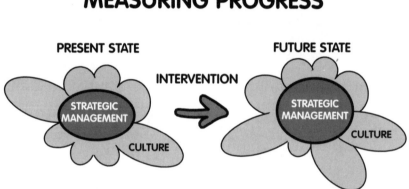

3.6.2 Scoring and Using the Assessment

One major problem of constructing an assessment is that it's very difficult to distinguish content from process. Let's give an example. Communism and Catholicism are both "order" paradigms. Why? They both distinguish right from wrong. The theme is very different but the scheme is the same.

If you filled out the assessment on pages 68-72, refer back to it now. The assessment test will give you an indication of the paradigms you are using the most. Remember, this is not a test of who you are, but of what values paradigms you use most frequently to handle your environment.

> *People adopt values that help them handle their environment. Using values as a base is then a way to cope with external pressure.*

Now write numbers sequentially in "Column 2" from 1 to 8 – over again and again. Like this: 1,2,3,4,5,6,7,8, 1,2,3,4,5,6,7,8, 1... A few numbers are there already. If you do not hit them right, go back and check it!

Count how many times you placed an "x" in front of the different numbers and write down the totals here. (Fourteen is the maximum for each category.)

Number in column 2	Graves Type	Your score (how many times have you put an "x" at that number)
1	Order	
2	Learning	
3	Power	
4	People	
5	Network	
6	Safety	
7	Achievement	
8	Survival	

You probably will display two or three high scores along with some lower scores. The number of x's is insignificant; the distribution is what is most relevant.

Evaluate for yourself what paradigms you are using in different situations. Some of the people we tested were amazed that they did not score high on paradigms that they felt had been a large part of their life. It might be from the "people" paradigm—having been from the '60's generation and lived in communes in their younger days. The reason why they do not score high, of course, is that this is not the way they handle life anymore. Their self-concept still keeps this image of being people-oriented even if they now almost entirely cope in other ways. What happens is that they are still able to draw on their "people" paradigm when needed, but it's not active at the moment.

Ask your colleagues to fill out the assessment and then discuss your scores. You may be able to improve your mutual cooperation by knowing what paradigms in which you and your peers operate.

3.7 Useful Hints

Let's recapture the possibilities of understanding and diagnosing the paradigms.

First of all, the paradigms permit you to "climb the tree" for perspective (as the lumberjacks on page 19) and get a general feeling for the predominant belief systems within the organization.

Second, they permit you to introduce tools consistent with the dominant paradigms. If a change in values and beliefs is necessary to prepare for implementation of certain tools, they give you the power to analyze the path to create new paradigms.

In mergers and acquisitions this could prove extremely useful. Most of the time there is a confrontation between two competing cultures.

Third, they offer the opportunity to create the culture in your organization that supports internal commitment and meets the needs of the market.

Fourth, they offer you personal insight to analyze others' exposed values and thereby connect with them in their belief system. This can be applied in whatever relationships you desire—for sales, for commitment, for friendship.

Chapter 4

Creating Shared Vision

The following seven chapters describe the environmental conditions necessary for obtaining congruence and alignment within organizations. Each of these seven areas could potentially be a book in its own right. What we want to do, though, is limit the focus to interesting viewpoints, basic beliefs supporting the themes, and connections to congruence and alignment.

4.1 Visions and Values

What is the problem with many visions? Quite often, no one pays attention to them. Many organizations don't even have one, and those who do can't find a way to gain committed to them. In this chapter we will look particularly into the problem of commitment to visions.

First, let's define vision.

> *Visions are expressions about future states that you or the organization want to be in.*

Remember section 2.2.1. the levels of values? Vision is establishing what's important to the business. That's the middle level of values.

THE VALUES LEVELS IN DETAIL

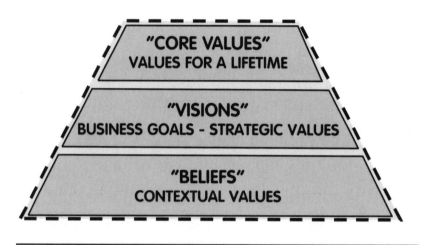

"CORE VALUES"
VALUES FOR A LIFETIME

"VISIONS"
BUSINESS GOALS - STRATEGIC VALUES

"BELIEFS"
CONTEXTUAL VALUES

Building shared vision is a values process.

In the previous chapter, we proposed that values also represent states to be in. It then follows that visions are values that you want to have in the future. Visions are the proactive way of striving for future congruence.

Visions are states in which you hope to be congruent in the future.

4.1.1 Making Sense

Have you seen vision statements like:

✔ "We will have an environment where people are valued."
✔ "We will have satisfied customers."

Try to negate them, and you will have the following:

✔ "We will not have an environment where people are valued."
✔ "We will not have satisfied customers."

Do they make sense? No. When the opposite does not make sense, then the original statement does not either. Nothing has a meaning without its opposite.

What makes sense is something that represents a choice. In other words, the opposite must also make sense as a choice for a vision statement to be valid. Here are examples:

✔ "We are going to build a new division for selling cars..."
✔ "We are going to implement the latest technology in the area of..."

> *Statements that do not have any meaning when stated in the opposite form do not in themselves have any meaning.*

The first trap to fall in is to create meaningless vision statements.

4.1.2 Creating Future State

Thinking further about this, let's clarify some principles.

First, try to imagine that you are going to buy a Saab. You have not seen many around. However, what happens now with your perception?

You see more Saab's than you ever dreamed. There really aren't more Saab's around—the difference is that you see them.

> *If something preoccupies you, it changes your perception.*

Normally, you can count on your perception unconsciously working with seven things (plus or minus two) at a time. All of them affect what you sense from the outside world. Things that are not important are disregarded for more pressing things.

(You have probably noticed that colleagues who are in love seem to use six of their available channels on their love interest—leaving almost only one channel for their work!)

Let's try something else.

Do not think of kangaroos, especially not the ones in Australia, jumping on the plains with small kangaroos sitting in their pouches.

What happens now? Your mind pictures kangaroos even though we told you not to.

The mind can only think about something. It cannot "not think" about something.

You might even know that from the expression: "Don't look back unless you want to go that way."

Let's go back to vision. Look at the figure on the next page.

Many companies start with "present state" to form a vision. They call for a retreat and bring in experts to tell about today's difficult market conditions. After that, they all gather in groups to discuss present problems, weaknesses and strengths. They focus on conflicts between departments, production problems and the lack of financial resources.

Now they are ready for visions. Or, are they? After having filled their minds with kangaroos in abundance, hardly any channels are left for the future state. All they see in the months to come will be proof of all of the problems they listed together. Surely they have production problems. Surely competition is tremendously difficult.

CREATING VISION

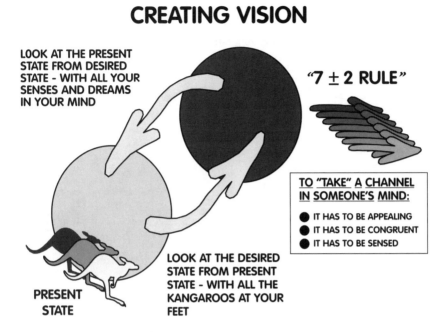

LOOK AT THE PRESENT STATE FROM DESIRED STATE - WITH ALL YOUR SENSES AND DREAMS IN YOUR MIND

"7 ± 2 RULE"

TO "TAKE" A CHANNEL IN SOMEONE'S MIND:

● IT HAS TO BE APPEALING
● IT HAS TO BE CONGRUENT
● IT HAS TO BE SENSED

LOOK AT THE DESIRED STATE FROM PRESENT STATE - WITH ALL THE KANGAROOS AT YOUR FEET

PRESENT STATE

The alternative is to start with desired state. What we want is to make an expression of a future state that we want to be in. Therefore, start your meetings with creativity and proactivity. Where do we want to be? How can we describe that in such a way that it "occupies" one of the available channels in people's minds?

We hear about possible collaboration with external partners. We look into project ideas. We envision the funding that will come to us from numerous sources when they hear the splendid results that our product will deliver. We see old products revitalized, and so on.

This works in a different way. In the coming months we will then read articles, meet people and see opportunities that permit things to happen. The vision is going to come true.

The outside world has not changed by associating into desired state. Your perception has.

OPTIMIST / PESSIMIST

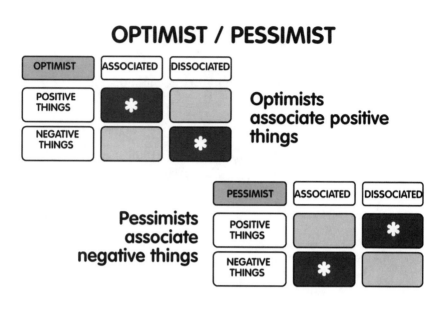

Optimists associate positive things

Pessimists associate negative things

Some people might say that this is not right. The problems have not disappeared. We have to address them. Look at the figure above. They have a tendency to associate problems and disassociate the positive.

Of course the problems are still there. If you solve them with your visions in mind, however, you will find solutions to move forward that you cannot perceive if you try to solve them with your present state in mind.

> We have been taught to believe that negative equals realistic and positive equals unrealistic.
>
> – Susan Jeffers

You are not going to get very far without being able to associate into desired state. To do that, you have to make a sensory rich representation of that state.

But how do you do that? How do you get hold of other people's subconscious "channels"?

First, the future state (vision) has to be appealing. That is, it must represent values and state that the majority of the organization sees as energizing. It's probably not appealing to make money if that money goes to enlarge other people's possibilities, but not your own.

One can describe it as "creative tension," or the difference between where you are and where you want to go. Think of a rubber band between the current and the desired state. If it is too loose (too easily obtained), it does not pull you toward the desired state. If it is too tight (too difficult or distant), it may break—not getting you there at all and disabling you in the process.

Second, the vision has to be congruent. Not only the vision itself, but also the way to get there. For example, having great visions doesn't really impact reality if resources to get there are not allocated.

And third, it has to be sensory rich. The way to do that is to create something to associate or link it with. Here are a couple of stories to illustrate.

With one client, we chose to create a story called, "A Day in the Life of Ann Smith—May 2000. It was a story of how self-directed work groups of non-skilled factory labor were to work in three years. The work group filled in lots of things that she participated in, trying to paint a rich job with lots of participation.

At first, management did not approve of the story. They needed the character to complete a particular degree of production during the day. Then we revised it to be "One Week in the Life of Ann Smith—May 2000" and management approved!

Then, we handed it to the shop stewards. They claimed that no shop stewards were mentioned in the story. "Well," we said, "We did not imagine any shop stewards, but if you would like, please write yourselves into the story." So they did.

Next, we gave the story to the skilled labor. They claimed that they were not in the story, either. They got the same answer as the shop stewards. So, they wrote themselves into the story.

At last we published the story for 3,800 unskilled workers with instructions for a debate. And every one of them debated it.

Telling the story made the difference. Now everyone had the vision of how it was going to work.

Here is a second case story.

One of our clients had a four-year plan. In trying to explain it, they composed the press release that they envisioned sending out after the four years.

It was a government office, and they had very long turnaround times for expediting work—about 9 months. They planned to implement technology and cut down lead time to less than three months. They had a hard time trying to get the staunchest pessimists to accept that it was feasible.

Two years later, they attained the whole plan. As everyone now knew what was going to happen, they felt no need to wait. They sat down for the second time to determine if response times could be reduced to one week!

Here is one more:

One client decided to give every employee a 36-exposure film and ask everyone to take pictures of what they thought would be worthwhile to achieve. They covered the office walls with pictures and held an event where people told about their pictures and aspirations.

Other options would be to make hand-drawn pictures, write a play, write songs or even to make your own television show from your visions.

> When you want to build a ship, don't begin by gathering wood or delegating tasks. Rather, increase the desire for the wide open sea.
>
> *—origin unknown*

Use whatever will catch the channels in people's minds.

> **Beware of FUN-phobia—it's better to get there laughing than to get nowhere bored.**

4.2 Vision and Values in Complex Systems

Vision processes are key factors for alignment. This is not only true for simple systems, but also in more complex systems.

In Section 1.2.2 we briefly mentioned the example of traffic. Let's look again at this system.

Traffic is controlled by very simple rules on a low level. "Don't bump into others" is basically all that is needed.

That is not all there is to it, however. When people are able to do that on a reliable basis, we put yet another system on top of it. These are laws that apply to traffic. Rules determine speed limits, who has right of way in given situations, and so on. The laws provide safe boundaries for the lower level system.

On top of that, we provide an infrastructure. This includes roads to drive on—one way streets, highways and ramps. The infrastructure puts additional parameters on traffic.

There's more. In addition, we put in place environmental and safety restrictions. Cars that are not safe to drive are banned. Cars that excessively pollute are ruled out, and so on.

On top of that, in many places there are taxes assessed on roads, gas, and so on. Each of these layers influences lower level behavior.

No one is trying to control every movement of traffic. There are, however, a lot of higher level systems setting parameters and expectations for lower level behavior.

What do we learn here?

Complex systems do not lend themselves to control on the lowest level. They are controlled in "layers." The basic principle is to make one layer at a time function before adding a new one on top.

CONTROLLED COMPLEXITY
-- each level sets the boundaries for the next level

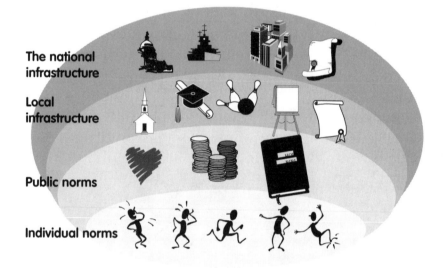

The national infrastructure

Local infrastructure

Public norms

Individual norms

The reliability of the lowest levels determines the quality of the system.

Controlling complex distributed systems on higher levels relies on simple systems that already work.

How do you put that to work in your organization?

One productive observation is that in your organization the lowest level is the individual, so the place to begin with is the people.

Getting it right for people means getting it right for more complex organizational behavior. So this is our system:

ALIGNING THE ORGANIZATION

ORGANIZATION

DIVISION

DEPARTMENT

TEAM

PEOPLE

THE LOWEST LEVEL IN COMPLEX
SYSTEMS IS PEOPLE

To control complexity you have to make your way through the system by following the logic of congruence and alignment. Enable people to work first. Attend to individual logical levels.

When individuals work properly; that is, when they feel **congruent,** create departmental **alignment** and let it serve as a guide for the individual system.

When departments work properly; that is, when they work **congruently,** create divisional **alignment** and let it serve as a guide for the departmental system.

When divisions work **congruently,** turn to **alignment** for the organization. When the organization works **congruently,** turn to **alignment** with the local environment. When the environment works **congruently**, turn to **alignment** with cyberspace or whatever your context might be—whatever number of layers you find appropriate.

This is also how it works in society. The layers in society are local municipalities, states and the federal government. When higher levels try to impose direct behavior controls on lower levels, things tend to break down. The federal government is seldom the most qualified to dictate local behavior.

Many companies try to direct values and visions from the top level, hoping for a cascading process of values and visions down through the organization. One reason why this approach often fails is that it is not followed by any real pursuit of congruence on all levels.

On the contrary, top management implements other control procedures on a behavior level to establish classical behavior control. This reduces the whole process to yet another behavioral management fix.

Major attempts to impose behavioral rules on lower levels without aligning values and identity will make the system tend to move more slowly, become less adaptive and less creative.

Vision and values processes in complex systems are established in layers. Each layer must be congruent and in alignment with the layer above.

If you disregard the importance of congruence for the individuals working for you, you will have no chance to ever get the more complex system to work.

Chapter 5
Creating Understanding

One of our clients has three different sales districts. They had a system in place to increase sales by encouraging internal competition between the districts. At one point, the prize offered was a trip to Bermuda for two.

One salesman learned about a large potential customer who planned to open a shop in the next district. This salesman could have contacted his colleague in that district to inform him of the opportunity. To do so, however, would have hurt his chances for winning the competition.

He won the prize all right. He and his wife had a wonderful week in Bermuda.

But the customer was lost. No one got around to contacting him.

We told this story at a later conference for the sales division in the company. (We got the permission, of course!) Most of the sales people reported that they would have done the same thing.

–Bjarne

If people are not aligned on a values level, they must follow the rules of behavior. This sometimes leads to the most terrible results.

Creating understanding leads to alignment. Let's look into that.

You have probably seen the film "Mission Impossible." In the opening scene the hero receives a small disk, hears the message and the magic words of suspense: "You will be kept informed on a need-to-know basis. This disk will now "self-destruct."

Information on a "need-to-know basis" is limiting. If information is kept to a minimum of behavioral instructions, the ability to align with company values deteriorates.

> One business leader publicly boasted about what he called his "No Shit" management style. He was proud of the fact that people in his organization only received information that they NEEDED to know. Emphasis was also placed on sticking to business—no unrelated topics were to be discussed.
>
> They made headlines when people experienced mental breakdowns and had to be hospitalized because of the terrible working climate.

LOGICAL LEVELS OF CHANGE FOR THE ORGANIZATION

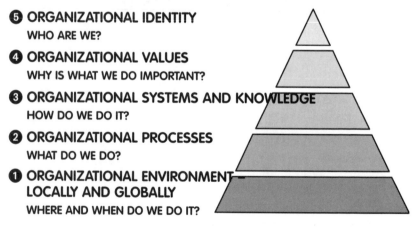

❺ ORGANIZATIONAL IDENTITY
WHO ARE WE?

❹ ORGANIZATIONAL VALUES
WHY IS WHAT WE DO IMPORTANT?

❸ ORGANIZATIONAL SYSTEMS AND KNOWLEDGE
HOW DO WE DO IT?

❷ ORGANIZATIONAL PROCESSES
WHAT DO WE DO?

❶ ORGANIZATIONAL ENVIRONMENT
LOCALLY AND GLOBALLY
WHERE AND WHEN DO WE DO IT?

Consider the figure on the previous page. Truly understanding the organization means understanding each of the levels.

In this chapter, we are going to focus on psychological consequences of understanding and aligning on a day-to-day basis.

5.1 Understanding Improves Working Relationships

Playing With a Full Deck

In one organization, we conducted sessions with a department that had three types of positions—A,B,C. We asked people in roles of A and B to explain the responsibilities of C. Then we asked C's to respond by confirming or denying the description given, as well as adding anything that was not mentioned. We repeated this process for each of the job categories. Many were surprised to learn what their colleagues actually accomplished during the day!

If you don't have an understanding of what work is done, you won't be playing with a full deck!

THE BARRIERS OF THE ORGANIZATION

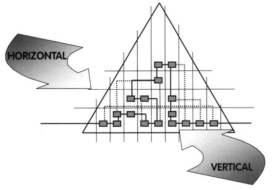

© *Scandinavian Training Design*

It's more common than not that people do not really know what's going on—even in their nearest neighborhood.

In general terms, organizations to a large extent are still organized in a hierarchical structure. The figure on the previous page illustrates the fact that informal and formal layers dominate most organizations, thereby impeding flexibility and understanding.

IMPROVING WORKING RELATIONSHIPS - CARING FOR PEOPLE

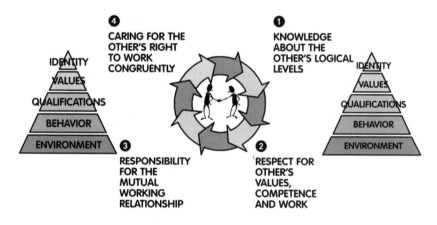

There is a basic mechanism here to consider.

In most organizations, suggestions for improvements are suggestions for other people to improve, not yourself. Obviously, it's a lot easier to consider other people as needing to change than yourself. But working relationships and cooperation do not thrive by considering colleagues incompetent. The remedy is knowledge. Knowing about people creates respect. It turns out that they, too, are working hard with good intentions.

Respect for other people's congruence is the key to taking responsibility. Not responsibility for others, of course, but for the working relationship you have with them. Taking responsibility means in the end "caring"—caring for others' working conditions.

This is really a spiral as this in turn creates even better working conditions, and so on. The implication of this is that:

> *To initiate and maintain "nice-to-know" information leads to better overall working relationships.*

5.2 The Day-to-Day Alignment Process

One reasonable way to address these issues is by focusing on the basic building block of business processes. In Total Quality Management (TQM), this is actually the key concept. You try to describe the essential business processes and make them the focal point of management. Simple flowcharts that give everyone a basic understanding can be of great value.

Making flowcharts for understanding is great. In a world of many words, visuals give people another way to understand. The problem arises when managers are so taken by their success in creating understandable flowcharts that they turn the process descriptions into instructions and rules for behavior. This, we may now know, is precisely the wrong thing to do, as rules for behavior (even visual ones!) do not in the end produce the desired result.

In essence, the problem is that no process description can account for the complicated network of communication and interaction that occurs in a company. Thus, the flowchart is only a dim reflection of reality.

> *A flowchart is great for understanding—and often a disaster for controlling.*

People making requests from each other and making promises coordinate almost all organizational service activities. ("Can you deliver this?" "I will pay that amount in ten days.")

So, on a detailed level another approach is more appropriate for alignment. A proven method is to let everyone enter into specific alignment discussions with each person that he or she interacts with. Everyone is at the same time customer and provider for others in the organization. Exchanging the personal logical levels perspective means knowing values, competence and agreed mutual behavior in the relationship. This works for teams as well.

By becoming an observer of yourself and others, you gain an understanding of the tremendous influence you have on co-creating your work environment. Trust, commitment and understanding are built through a series of small steps—eventually affecting the way a work group aligns to the company values and vision.

Individual to Individual Alignment

Basic alignment occurs when a request or offer is made, is mutually understood, and is then carried out as expected by the person who made the request. It involves:

- Shared **values** and visions

- Understanding of needed **competence/qualifications**, as related to the actual issue and to process communication skills

- Agreement on ground rules for **behavior**

- A decision to trust others to be congruent in values and behavior

Misalignments—or breakdowns—occur when there are differences between what was understood as requested, what the options were, and what was supposed to be carried out.

- Unexpressed intentions

- Inaccurate inferences about the other party's relationship between behavior and intentions

5.3 Understanding Flow

Knowing the company processes and getting relationships in place are part of a pattern of understanding. One more aspect is important—understanding the nature of organizational dynamics. Think of a mobile. Each of the items hangs in a delicate balance. Pull on one of the strings, and the whole creation shifts in response to the change. So it is with our organizations. Systems have an affect on each other. As the saying goes, "one thing leads to another."

In his younger days, Finn was employed by a company dealing with dentists. As part of his work, he participated in Dentist Specialist training. One of the topics was how to build fixtures to hold a set of dentures.

One simple principle was taught: Never affix the whole thing to more than two permanent teeth. If you affix it to three, inevitably one of the fix points will loosen and the tooth will come out.

Some dentists learned that their approach of doing something extra for their customers (fixing the denture at an extra point at no extra expense) was really a subtle way of removing all of their clients' teeth in ten year's time!

Think about what would happen if one of the mobile pieces was "nailed" into place. As the rest of the mobile responded to the environment, what would happen? Tension would result. The "fixed" element would potentially lose its relationship to the whole. The mobile would lose its flexibility and adaptability.

So things may react unexpectedly. We have to keep it this way if we want adaptability and flexibility. You keep maximum influence by not fixing things into rules.

You actually influence a system by being flexible—not by nailing things in place!

Finn tells this story from his time as a production manager at on a large steel manufacturing plant. This was certainly an environment for planning, if any.

Sometimes someone missed work on a particular day due to illness or other perfectly valid reason. This was a serious matter. I learned that these cases often were sent to the top of the organization. People waited for me to make some sort of decision on moving resources from one sector to another. At the very beginning, this was then what I did.

But to my surprise this maneuver often lead to problems almost doubling the size of the original problem in the department that was short only one person. In essence, they seemed to miss two. Covering up for that new problem in turn created a hole in production of four and so on. In less than a day, the whole factory was disrupted.

The lesson learned was that strict central planning and low redundancy leads to low adaptability.

I solved this by enabling each department to use more flexible planning. They were encouraged to solve problems of that size for themselves. By loosening control, the flow of work and higher production were maintained.

This insight is hard to grasp for managers as well as employees. That's because of our belief in cause and effect. Leaving it means entering a new age.

A small hole in the bottom of a sink can change the way the whole body of water flows.

No one group can know the whole system. Each individual, team, and department can handle the local situation by following a few simple rules. Just as a human body exchanges every cell in a span of seven years—it is most important that the pattern be preserved, but not necessarily the physical matter itself.

> To understand how a human body functions, you would not spread all of the pieces before you—a heart here, a lung there, an ear in the middle... Comprehension of the functions comes by watching the interaction of the systems. A whole organism is more than the sum of its parts.

Understanding the system means to understand the value of the informal structure and the hidden pathways.

That is why we have to reorganize our thinking about control.

> *These informal structures will work for you at maximum efficiency if you use congruence and alignment.*
>
> *They may disappear or work counterproductively if you work with traditional control of behavior.*

5.4 Information Flow

There are many other ways to accomplish information exchange. Examples are meetings, seminars, cross-training opportunities, electronic communications, and network forums, even pagers and cell phones! Or simply, eliminating barriers to the natural knowledge pathways that people tend to form.

An excellent approach is to create redundancy in information systems. One common principal for important information is to "send the message seven times—and seven different ways." It is not enough to communicate a complex message once and expect that everyone has understood the idea. Try to find a variety of means to tell the story, including—visually (let people have a look at it) auditory (how does it sound) and kinesthetically (let people get a feeling for it).

> We had a client (a regional union office for nurses) who proudly showed us their annual report detailing their activi-

ties. It consisted of 45 pages with very small letters. As written messages are not the preferred strategy for most nurses, and 45 pages of small letters hardly is the strategy for anyone—they did not accomplish very much toward the goal of getting information to the members with this approach.

Whatever you do, remember:

> *Essentially, nice-to-know information is the fuel that feeds the process of alignment.*

5.5 Getting the Market to Understand

Understanding your role in a network of partners and customers is part of the whole theme of understanding.

Let's refer back to section 1.2.4 about network economics. Think of your customers as part of the organization. The traditional approach of trying to influence behavior by advertising corresponds to classical marketing.

DIFFERENT MARKETING STYLES
- INTO NETWORK ECONOMICS

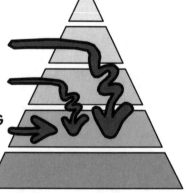

MARKETING THROUGH VALUES
Creating add-on value of your product

MARKETING THROUGH LEARNING
Creating a path to your product

MARKETING THROUGH ADVERTISING
Classical marketing

If you view the marketing process as being an alignment process of customers to the company, you must consider all of the logical levels as a whole.

Using values in marketing has been a method for the past 20 years. There are many examples of appeals to lifestyle.

Using the qualifications level by applying the concept of creating a path and teaching customers to purchase your product are techniques from the '90's and beyond. To be able to tap the power of both—values and path creation—imagine the impact!

Chapter 6

Creating Learning

> I used to get into long debates with a friend. We thought very differently about a number of issues. At a certain point, he would turn to me and say, "Here is your perception of how things are..." Then he would attempt to repeat my point of view. After that, he would say, "Now, here's how things *are...*" My friend recognized that I had a personal perception of a situation, but thought he OWNED reality!
>
> *– Arlene*

This chapter will address the essential factors that affect learning. From the logical levels perspective, it is about management directed toward the qualification level.

On the personal level, it's about the ability to stay congruent. As personal logical levels are dynamically evolving and the alignment process is ongoing, no one stays congruent without the ability to change. People therefore need to keep learning. They need to be able to change for themselves.

6.1 The Learning Cycle

Learning in the workplace environment basically follows Kolb's Learning Cycle.

THE ORGANIZATION'S LEARNING CYCLE

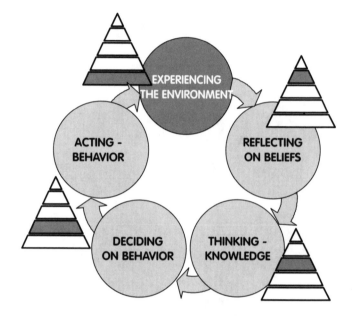

The learning cycle was originally intended for application to individuals. However, it also applies to groups. Most people learn in this way, and we will show how it is possible to instill this process as a shared culture for collective learning. This is the learning/systemic approach.

Many use the learning cycle in their professional life. Doctors diagnose, treat and get feedback. Teachers prepare, teach and get feedback. Researchers plan experiments, perform them and get feedback. But do they also use the learning cycle as part of their whole culture? Do they learn from all the other things they participate in such as meetings, presentations, administrative work, projects and so on?

To create that kind of culture, a general perspective of learning and development must be established. Graves' "learning" values will be a useful paradigm.

As previously indicated, the issue here is how to create a culture for accelerating learning on a personal and collective level. This is done by replacing counterproductive beliefs.

6.2 The Values Behind Learning

Many managers never quite understood that establishing a learning organization means that they themselves must know something about learning.

This is by no means a comprehensive book about learning. We just want to touch on some especially important models. Models are important because they constitute a basic belief system about others and our own learning. This dramatically affects our organizations.

So, they are not just techniques, but also productive belief systems relevant for creating congruence and alignment.

6.1.1 The Map of the World

One of the first and most basic assumptions in learning (and communication) is the concept of "The Map of the World." People do not perceive the same thing whenever they experience the same event. An important distinction is that "The Map is not the Territory" (my view is not the only "reality").

People perceive through filters. A simple test is to place a simple dust pan in the middle of the floor and ask a group of people questions about it:
 ✔ Is it large or small?
 ✔ Is it pretty or ugly?
 ✔ Is it wide or narrow?
 ✔ Is it white or gray?
 ✔ and so on...

Ask ten questions and no one will have the same ten answers. To an extent, we simply create our own inner reality.

People also have preferences in modalities. That is, some people feel most comfortable when they see things, some people when they hear them and some people when they feel them. We use all of our senses, but some of them work better for us than others. This is called our preferred representation system.

If you want to create learning, congruence and alignment, respecting the fact that people have different preferences becomes essential.

BARRIERS TO THE INDIVIDUAL

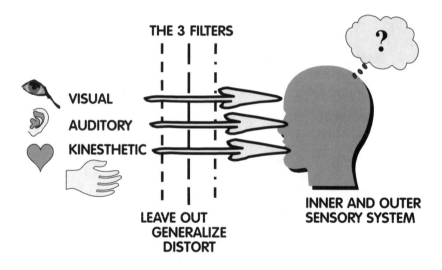

THE 3 FILTERS

VISUAL
AUDITORY
KINESTHETIC

LEAVE OUT
GENERALIZE
DISTORT

INNER AND OUTER
SENSORY SYSTEM

You have to make a sensory-rich environment where all representation systems are present. No single representation will reach everyone.

A second learning point is that:

> *The belief that there is no such thing as one reality—only a perceived reality—might be the largest break-through for many organizations. We are constantly in the process of co-creating our reality.*

This is of vital importance. Accepting this as a belief makes tremendous differences in how situations are perceived and approached. We have found that acceptance of this simple assumption is one of the single most powerful factors for changing organizational cultures. Try it out.

If you meet a person who believes his perceived reality is more accurate than yours, what would he most likely do? He would try to influence your way of seeing things.

If you meet a person who is aware that "The map is not the territory" (my perception is not the only "reality"), what would he possibly do? He would ask about your point of view.

Which one would you rather meet? Are you yourself the kind of person others want to meet?

To accept this means that you must suspend any automatic assumption about connections between behavior and intent. People's behavior (however strange it might seem to you) could be based on positive intentions that you cannot imagine because they do not exist in your "map of the world."

You simply have to ask. Be curious about other people, and forget all about interpreting. It is difficult—yes—but most rewarding for the relationships you have with people.

> *Don't get angry—get curious. Ask!*

6.1.2 Different Kinds of Intelligence

People are not only different in perception; they also work differently with the data they take in. One of the most rewarding frameworks to use is Howard Gardner's model of eight intelligences. There are three books on this subject referenced in the literature list. They are written by Howard Gardner, Linda Campell, et. al., and David Lazear.

EIGHT TYPES OF INTELLIGENCE

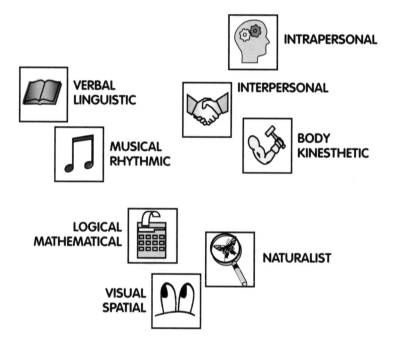

The short story is that people who are predominantly:

✔ **verbal/linguistic,** are best at reading and writing, speaking, debate and humor.

✔ **musical/rhythmic,** are best at tonal patterns, music, vibrations, singing and pacing.

✔ **logical mathematical,** are best at symbols, sequences, logic, patterns, numbers and problem solving.

✔ **visual/spatial,** are best at design, painting, pictures, drawings, mind-mapping and active imagination.

✔ **naturalists,** are best at nature, classification of species, biological observations, plants and other nature experiences.

✔ **body/kinesthetic,** are best at physical activity, sports, role playing, invention of things and dance.

✔ **interpersonal,** are best at intuitively sensing others' feelings, giving feedback, person-to-person communication, collaboration, and teamwork.

✔ **intrapersonal,** are best at internal reflection, getting into contact with their own feelings, concentration and personal independence.

As you may have noticed, Logical/Mathematical or Verbal/ Linguistic Intelligence is traditional intelligence. We have accepted it for a century since Binet invented the IQ. With Howard Gardner and recently Daniel Goleman's "Emotional Intelligence" we are finally acknowledging a more differentiated view of intelligence.

We will not go futher into this here. You can read the literature for yourself, but some major points are valuable.

> *Believing that people can be intelligent in many different ways is a major breakthrough in many organizations.*

When we have taught this, some participants have realized for the first time that they are intelligent according to their preferred intelligence. Some were so accustomed to being evaluated according to traditional intelligence measures that they almost gave up. What such a discovery means for anyone's self-esteem and beliefs about his or her own learning is incredible.

The tolerance and appreciation for others that also comes with it is valuable, too. It is the same story as "The Map of the World." We are certainly different. We have different contributions to make toward our shared reality.

In team learning, this perspective is highly productive. Everyone measures which preferences they possess. Then their colleagues guess their dominant intelligence type. Some teams are very accurate. But sometimes teams get huge surprises—realizing that they did not have a clue about other team members' learning strategies.

6.3 Using Creativity and Mental Jogging

The last suggestion is to implement "mental jogging." By that, we mean that creativity and breaking assumptions are activities that can be strengthened through use in the same way that endurance is increased by physical jogging.

> *To do that, break any FUN-phobia assumptions or you will never get to it. Mental jogging is fun!*

One way to foster creativity is to create an environment where people bring in **strange and thought provoking items and problems.** Some of these are small brain teasers based on breaking small assumptions where the mind generalizes too quickly.

Here is one: On the next page is a swimming pool with four trees in the corners. The family has grown. The pool needs to be doubled in size, but still a square. How would you do it?

There are at least five reasonable solutions. Can you find them? Some possible answers are in the back of the book.

There is another interesting technique called **failure systems.** The idea is that you take time out to come together and ask for something that is more or less impossible, such as, "How do we double our sales in two weeks?"

THE POOL

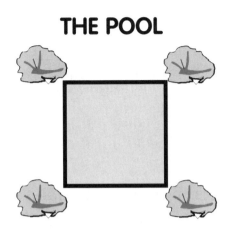

The psychology of this is that any suggestion most likely is insufficient or crazy. But that does not matter. One does not lose status among peers because of that. On the contrary.

The point is that this not only serves as a mental jogging exercise, but from time to time very good ideas pop up and constitute valuable input for business.

One additional way to provoke creativity is to introduce a **perceived loss of control.** The way to do that is to imagine something worse. Doing that provokes creativity to regain control and thereby brings out more solutions for the problem.
An example could be:

If you are short three people in the office you have a problem. But what if you were missing seven? What would you do then? You could most likely find additional solutions to the original problem.

The final suggestion is to use **association techniques.** Bring something different into the situation and combine it with whatever you have. New combinations foster creativity.

> *Mental jogging is paving the way for improved learning and the breaking of counterproductive beliefs.*

Chapter 7

Creating Self-Esteem

Self-esteem is the next major factor in creating an environment for cultural change.

Sometimes we are at a very small conference center with our management groups. One particular center only has 17 rooms. Rikke, who owns the center, normally does not care whether you take one room or another. As all rooms are unique, you take what is available when you arrive.

One more feature of this place is a central paging system with a loudspeaker in every room. Rikke normally uses it for calling people to breakfast.

One morning, though, she called (so everyone could hear it), "Finn, I do not know what room you are in, but the light at home is not working and your wife wants to know what she's supposed to do!"

In Danish homes, the fuses are installed centrally. The thing to do is replace the fuse. Finn's wife, however, had never done that before. He had taken care of this while we lived at this house.

This is called "learned helplessness" and is one sure way of lowering other people's self-esteem. As a leader you only have to take a job from an employee a few times before the consequence is that this employee has learned that he is not qualified for that job.

There is a continuation to this story.

Finn called his wife and told her that the hot fuse was the one to replace. She did it. No need to tell you that Finn was met with laughter later on at breakfast.

About six months later though, the loudspeaker was used again: "Finn, I do not know which room you are in, but the fuse has blown again—and none of the fuses are hot!"

A frustrated man called his spouse who was away on business. "How on earth do you get this washing machine to work? It won't fill up with water!" His spouse had always taken care of the laundry duties in this particular household. She knew it had been working when she left the house, so she started asking some questions. As it turned out, the machine he was attempting to use was the dryer!

Managers sometimes take on tasks that they should let people in the organization undertake. When this happens, they get things done more quickly—at least in the short run—but there is a problem. People do not learn how to do it for the next time. In addition, they get the message that they are not able to learn it at all.

> **"Learned helplessness" is a sure way to lower self-esteem.**

Self-esteem is one of the most important factors for developing an organization. Lack of self-esteem is a silent killer.

You cannot order it. You see the symptoms of the lack of it, however. One sure thing is that organizations and individuals without self-esteem do not perform, develop, and thrive.

Therefore, understanding it and nurturing it is of extreme importance for all of the other things to work well.

7.1 A Model for Self-Esteem

7.1.1 The Logical Levels

Let's look at what self-esteem really is. The model we present here was developed with our Norwegian partner, Karin Hjertaker. Look at the Logical Levels of Change model again. Let's interpret self-esteem according to the levels.

Self-esteem, in the basic sense, is the way you perceive yourself. In other words, it is what you think about yourself; your sense of identity which is the top logical level.

Following this track, to create self-esteem must be dependent on the levels below.

Just below are values. The first major component of self-esteem is being respected for your values. Disrespect for values is one of the most effective ways to destroy self-esteem.

SELF-ESTEEM

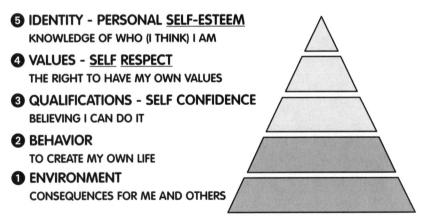

❺ IDENTITY - PERSONAL SELF-ESTEEM
KNOWLEDGE OF WHO (I THINK) I AM

❹ VALUES - SELF RESPECT
THE RIGHT TO HAVE MY OWN VALUES

❸ QUALIFICATIONS - SELF CONFIDENCE
BELIEVING I CAN DO IT

❷ BEHAVIOR
TO CREATE MY OWN LIFE

❶ ENVIRONMENT
CONSEQUENCES FOR ME AND OTHERS

Think of an organization where you are forced to do things you do not agree with—things that go against your values. It might be as simple as treating customers according to principles you do not believe in, or it might be taking on tasks out of fear for your job.

In many cases, the simple threat of being fired or being excluded from social acceptance are reasons enough to comply with the boss.

If you do only what others expect of you, you might feel a spinal "meltdown." You lose **self respect.**

The level below that is qualifications—the feeling of being competent. It is the second major building block for self-esteem. If you do not have the qualifications, you lose your **self-confidence.**

Too much self-confidence is, by the way, also a problem. Sometimes when you have people in a coaching session and are trying to boost their self-confidence, you might get into the "confidence/ competence trap." This happens when the coached person gets so excited that he loses his ability to evaluate himself realistically.

> **Self-esteem is built from self-respect and self-confidence.**

7.1.2 Building Self-Esteem

Let's look once more at the model.

We have added what is called "The Circle of Integration" for building positive self-esteem. The process starts with clarifying personal values, giving freedom of choice to choose one's own behavior and creating your identity. Remember, it's by your exposed behavior that other people will judge you.

Now, isn't it amazing that self-esteem is essentially built by the same process that leads to congruence?

It's simple. The crucial question: **"What is important about that?"** (Sec. 2.1.3) leads not only to congruence, but is the direct way of starting a positive process of building up self-esteem. Self-esteem is closely related to values. One leads to the other.

The same is true for organizations. If management does not clarify values, the organizational self-esteem erodes. The organization will not have the identity of being something special, and thereby misses the opportunity to use the power of alignment.

The acid test of people's concept of their organization would be a question like, "What do you do for a living?" Answers like, "I am an engineer," or "I work in an office," are not inspiring. Wouldn't you rather hear something like, "I work at ... that works in the field of... We are seeking to...and take care of...providing for the needs of ... We have special values about ... which is really our leverage point in the market, nobody else being ..."

THE CIRCLE OF INTEGRATION
- when self-esteem works

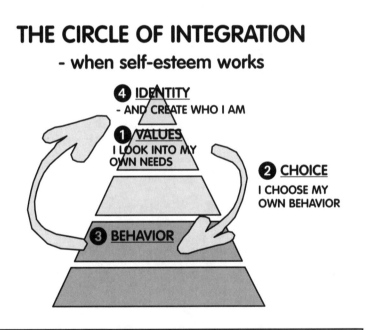

> *Organizations without visions and values lose self-esteem, thereby losing power to learn, adapt and perform.*

THE CIRCLE OF INTEGRATION
- when the organization's self-esteem works

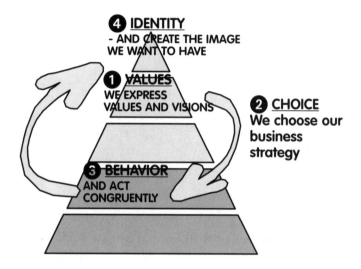

❹ IDENTITY
- AND CREATE THE IMAGE
WE WANT TO HAVE

❶ VALUES
WE EXPRESS
VALUES AND VISIONS

❷ CHOICE
We choose our
business
strategy

❸ BEHAVIOR
AND ACT
CONGRUENTLY

7.1.3 Caught in a Role

Sometimes we ask a group whether someone present would like to do something else in the organization—to use other skills. Almost without exception most of the people present indicate they would appreciate that opportunity.

Many people are kept in jobs to do tasks that they perform perfectly. They do not change because everyone thinks they are the most qualified to do that particular job.

In discussions of this topic, people are often amazed at what they hear from their colleagues. They respond, "I thought you really liked to do that. I never dreamed that you were bored by it for quite some time."

We have a strong tendency in organizations to keep people in roles where they perform well. We often don't recognize that many would like to get on with their life and take on the challenge of learning new skills.

THE CIRCLE OF INTEGRATION
- when I am caught by my own image

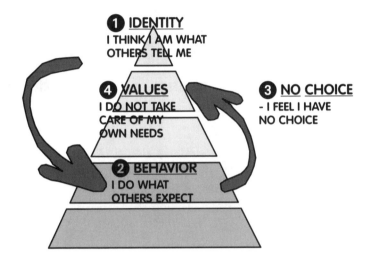

Take a look at the figure. Here is what happens. If the organization seeks to put people into boxes and roles, the circle might start to move the other way around. This creates the feeling of "no choice" and does not address values. It creates loss of self-esteem.

While you think that you are strengthening people by keeping them at what they can do well, one day it might no longer satisfy their needs. Self-esteem might start to erode.

7.1.4 When You Try to Live By Others' Values

How many times have you heard about other peoples' kids (not yours of course) who were forced to do something that their parents wanted more than they really wanted for themselves? How many times have you heard a manager say something like, "I really think it would be a great opportunity for you to take that seminar. By the way, I already booked it for you. You are registered to go to the September session."

Or, think of a time when people have been put into a position that they really did not want, but felt obliged to take.

THE CIRCLE OF INTEGRATION
- when others define my needs and values

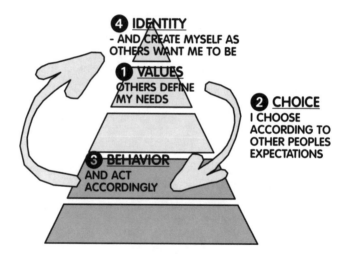

This time the figure shows that the circle is moving the right way, but it's not the person's own values that are addressed.

This is one more way to lose self-esteem.

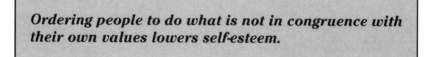

Ordering people to do what is not in congruence with their own values lowers self-esteem.

The same could happen for organizations. Being reactive in the market, trying to follow pressure and doing "what is needed from us" in a changing world can eventually lead to lower organizational self-esteem. Unfortunately, this will decreas ability to react to change, and thereby deepen the crisis.

This is illustrated by the next figure.

THE CIRCLE OF INTEGRATION
- when the organization is caught up in it's own image

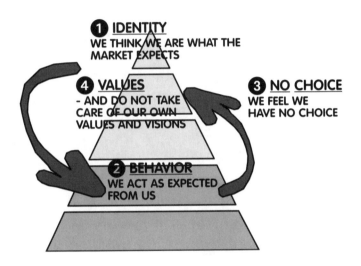

7.1.5 Managing for Self-Esteem

What can be done? Certainly, visions and values are an integral part. To address these, chapter four contains ideas.

There is also a daily component to this that is a management style issue. You have contact with people every day in the organization. Building self-esteem is not possible if you do not build it by the way you react to everyday situations. This means working on the three upper levels of your employees' logical levels. Address identity, values and qualifications instead of always staying at the behavior level.

TO CREATE SELF-ESTEEM

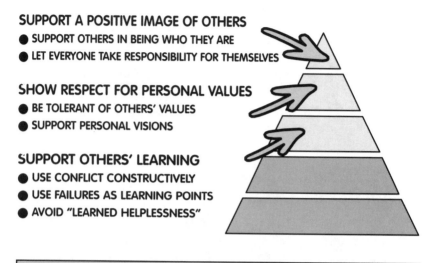

SUPPORT A POSITIVE IMAGE OF OTHERS
- SUPPORT OTHERS IN BEING WHO THEY ARE
- LET EVERYONE TAKE RESPONSIBILITY FOR THEMSELVES

SHOW RESPECT FOR PERSONAL VALUES
- BE TOLERANT OF OTHERS' VALUES
- SUPPORT PERSONAL VISIONS

SUPPORT OTHERS' LEARNING
- USE CONFLICT CONSTRUCTIVELY
- USE FAILURES AS LEARNING POINTS
- AVOID "LEARNED HELPLESSNESS"

> *Supporting self-esteem on a daily basis means to address the three upper logical levels.*

7.2 The Seven Habits Revisited

You probably know and appreciate Steven Covey's book, *Seven Habits of Highly Effective People*. To help you remember, one of the real insights of the book is that you cannot build **inter**dependence without having first built **in**dependence. So public victory follows from private victory.

Look at the figure below. We have put the first three habits into our model of self-esteem.

1. Be proactive
2. Begin with the end in mind
3. Put first things first

Adjusting the words slightly, they match the circle of integration for building personal self-esteem.

PERSONAL SELF-ESTEEM
The basis for
ORGANIZATIONAL SELF-ESTEEM

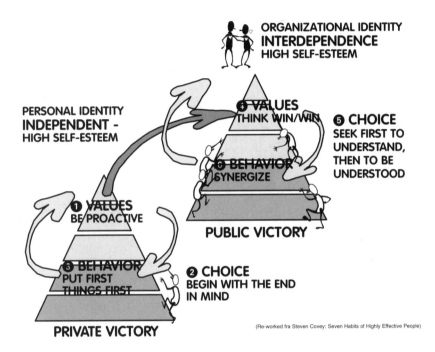

ORGANIZATIONAL IDENTITY
INTERDEPENDENCE
HIGH SELF-ESTEEM

PERSONAL IDENTITY
INDEPENDENT -
HIGH SELF-ESTEEM

④ VALUES
THINK WIN/WIN

⑤ CHOICE
SEEK FIRST TO
UNDERSTAND,
THEN TO BE
UNDERSTOOD

⑥ BEHAVIOR
SYNERGIZE

① VALUES
BE PROACTIVE

PUBLIC VICTORY

③ BEHAVIOR
PUT FIRST
THINGS FIRST

② CHOICE
BEGIN WITH THE END
IN MIND

PRIVATE VICTORY

(Re-worked fra Steven Covey: Seven Habits of Highly Effective People)

Then we have put the next three habits into the circle of integration
for organizational self-esteem.

4. Think win/win
5. Seek first to understand, then to be understood
6. Synergize

> *High organizational self-esteem emerges only when
> personal self-esteem is addressed.*

155

Chapter 8

Creating Cooperation

8.1 A Team Model

We have worked with teams for many years. One question frequently asked is: "What is a team? What is the real difference between individuals gathered in a group and a true team?"

The standard answers are something like **teams are characterized by:**

- ✔ A set of common goals
- ✔ Use of agreed methods
- ✔ Mutual beneficial interaction
- ✔ Use of everybody's abilities
- ✔ Clear division of roles

and more of the same category.

Many of these points are important—but what is the essential difference between a group of individuals and a true TEAM?

It now becomes clearer.

TEAMS BUILD ON RELATIONSHIPS

**GROUPS DO NOT NOT HAVE ALL OF
THEIR RELATIONSHIPS IN PLACE**

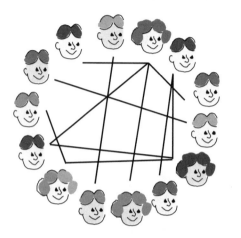

**TEAMS WORK LIKE ONE
UNIT - HAVING ALL THE
RELATIONSHIPS
ESTABLISHED**

> *Teams are built on relationships of trust.*

Relationships are obviously not just drinking beer with colleagues or participating in a game of darts. We are talking about professional relationships.

Take a closer look at the logical levels model once more. Creating a process where all of the levels of the model are discussed and clearly understood builds relationships. The process leads to mutual understanding of the group and the individual's potential within it.

Following these five steps constitutes a process that gets teams quickly up to speed.

One important feature in team building is the establishment of ground rules. They are behavioral norms on which the group agrees. They are based on ideas from the values level, but best expressed in behavioral terms. Here is an example:

"We respect each other."

This is not a helpful ground rule, as it is designating a value, but not how the value is expressed behaviorally. Each person translates for himself or herself what it means on the behavior level. To one it may mean calling out a greeting in the morning as people arrive. To another, it may mean dispensing with unnecessary interruptions (like greeting people as they come in!).

The most productive ground rules are rooted in values, but expressed on the behavior level. The rules then reflect the group's choice between different relevant behaviors.

A rule like, "We rotate responsibility for the facilitation of meetings among the members from meeting to meeting," is relevant because other solutions are also feasible.

GROUP CONGRUENCE

❺ GROUP IDENTITY
WHO ARE WE? WHAT ARE OUR INDIVIDUAL ROLES?

❹ GROUP VALUES AND BELIEFS
OUR VISIONS, GOALS AND COMMITMENT

❸ METHODS AND KNOWLEDGE
METHODS, MEETINGS, PLANNING, CONFLICT RESOLUTION

❷ GROUP BEHAVIOR
GROUND RULES - WALK THE TALK

❶ GROUP ENVIRONMENT
KEEPING ENERGY

8.2 Adding a Member

It is easy to overlook the fact that people join and leave the organization. Many team programs do not have a provision for taking on new members.

INTEGRATING A NEW MEMBER

A NEW MEMBER

THE OLD TEAM

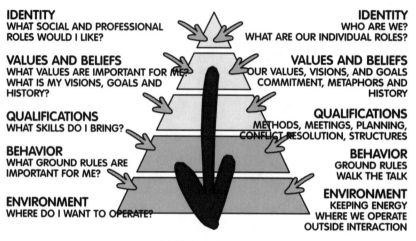

IDENTITY
WHAT SOCIAL AND PROFESSIONAL
ROLES WOULD I LIKE?

IDENTITY
WHO ARE WE?
WHAT ARE OUR INDIVIDUAL ROLES?

VALUES AND BELIEFS
WHAT VALUES ARE IMPORTANT FOR ME?
WHAT IS MY VISIONS, GOALS AND
HISTORY?

VALUES AND BELIEFS
OUR VALUES, VISIONS, AND GOALS
COMMITMENT, METAPHORS AND
HISTORY

QUALIFICATIONS
WHAT SKILLS DO I BRING?

QUALIFICATIONS
METHODS, MEETINGS, PLANNING,
CONFLICT RESOLUTION, STRUCTURES

BEHAVIOR
WHAT GROUND RULES ARE
IMPORTANT FOR ME?

BEHAVIOR
GROUND RULES
WALK THE TALK

ENVIRONMENT
WHERE DO I WANT TO OPERATE?

ENVIRONMENT
KEEPING ENERGY
WHERE WE OPERATE
OUTSIDE INTERACTION

OUR NEW TEAM

Think of a stable organization where everyone stays an average of seven years. If you work in a team-based organization, this means a turnover of 14%. This means any average-sized team in the organization must face integrating one new member each year. Even ad hoc teams often have members who come and go.

Adding a new member means building up relationships of trust again. The logical levels approach can be useful for getting on track—and fast—when integrating a new member.

8.3 Team Roles

You have probably seen many examples of team role systems. The most frequently used are Belbin's Roles and the Myers-Briggs Type Indicator based on Jung. The purpose of these models is to help people better understand the variety of behaviors represented in a group.

By doing this, it creates tolerance, as well as understanding of strengths and weaknesses. It even increases understanding for total group behavior, as some roles might be overrepresented while others are missing.

We have used the TMS (Team Management System), a Jung-based system. It is a fine tool and we will now apply the logical levels approach to that system.

© TMS
Charles Margerison and Dick McCann

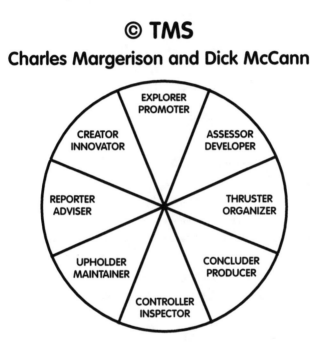

To be clear, we have to mention that this is just an unofficial demonstration of how to apply logical levels to any team role model. It is not a part of the TMS system. To learn more about the system, read the book by Margerison & McCann.

A good "fit" in a group involves all levels, not just behavior. By including all levels you increase your chance of creating a successful result.

One recommendation for implementation is to have team members map their preferences individually. Then, have a discussion together to increase understanding.

TEAM ROLES IN A LOGICAL LEVELS PERSPECTIVE

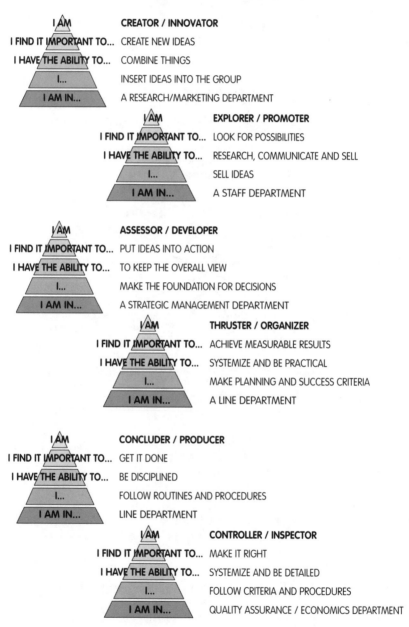

CREATOR / INNOVATOR

I AM

I FIND IT IMPORTANT TO... CREATE NEW IDEAS

I HAVE THE ABILITY TO... COMBINE THINGS

I... INSERT IDEAS INTO THE GROUP

I AM IN... A RESEARCH/MARKETING DEPARTMENT

EXPLORER / PROMOTER

I AM

I FIND IT IMPORTANT TO... LOOK FOR POSSIBILITIES

I HAVE THE ABILITY TO... RESEARCH, COMMUNICATE AND SELL

I... SELL IDEAS

I AM IN... A STAFF DEPARTMENT

ASSESSOR / DEVELOPER

I AM

I FIND IT IMPORTANT TO... PUT IDEAS INTO ACTION

I HAVE THE ABILITY TO... TO KEEP THE OVERALL VIEW

I... MAKE THE FOUNDATION FOR DECISIONS

I AM IN... A STRATEGIC MANAGEMENT DEPARTMENT

THRUSTER / ORGANIZER

I AM

I FIND IT IMPORTANT TO... ACHIEVE MEASURABLE RESULTS

I HAVE THE ABILITY TO... SYSTEMIZE AND BE PRACTICAL

I... MAKE PLANNING AND SUCCESS CRITERIA

I AM IN... A LINE DEPARTMENT

CONCLUDER / PRODUCER

I AM

I FIND IT IMPORTANT TO... GET IT DONE

I HAVE THE ABILITY TO... BE DISCIPLINED

I... FOLLOW ROUTINES AND PROCEDURES

I AM IN... LINE DEPARTMENT

CONTROLLER / INSPECTOR

I AM

I FIND IT IMPORTANT TO... MAKE IT RIGHT

I HAVE THE ABILITY TO... SYSTEMIZE AND BE DETAILED

I... FOLLOW CRITERIA AND PROCEDURES

I AM IN... QUALITY ASSURANCE / ECONOMICS DEPARTMENT

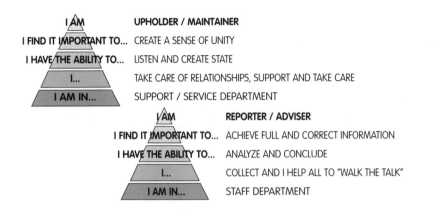

I AM — UPHOLDER / MAINTAINER

I FIND IT IMPORTANT TO... CREATE A SENSE OF UNITY

I HAVE THE ABILITY TO... LISTEN AND CREATE STATE

I... TAKE CARE OF RELATIONSHIPS, SUPPORT AND TAKE CARE

I AM IN... SUPPORT / SERVICE DEPARTMENT

I AM — REPORTER / ADVISER

I FIND IT IMPORTANT TO... ACHIEVE FULL AND CORRECT INFORMATION

I HAVE THE ABILITY TO... ANALYZE AND CONCLUDE

I... COLLECT AND I HELP ALL TO "WALK THE TALK"

I AM IN... STAFF DEPARTMENT

One additional thought. Do not confuse this with Graves' paradigms. These are individual preferences in team environments—roles. Graves' values paradigms are cultural characteristics that people adopt to handle different situations of life.

8.4 Self-Directed Work Teams – Management Beliefs

One of our friends is a match race sailor, and a girl. One summer, two boys and our friend went for special training, and they made a great team.

As the week progressed, they won everything—getting the flattering nickname of "The Dream Team" of the week.

Coming home, the skipper announced that from now on all the girls had to be removed from the team.

This was very confusing... How could he possibly mean that? What on earth could be the intention?

Digging into it, he had had his ambitions raised during that week of victory. He had decided that the climb to the top was not possible with girls on board.

What can we learn from this?

Could it be that team values did not truly have a high priority in this person's belief system as the initial behavior had seemed to indicate?

As it appears, the skipper's personal concept of how things are accomplished, his concept of girls in general, and other things totally overruled the fact that his success that week was rooted in true teamwork.

As a matter of fact, in our experience this is not so uncommon. Many managers have no internal reference for successful teamwork, and therefore have no deep beliefs connected with it. Teamwork is just another tool in a personal "achievement" paradigm, leading to personal victory.

This is why many often have a real hard time implementing team-based management.

On the other hand, most managers have a concept of good or bad management. Good management means "being in control of things, not letting feelings affect tough personnel decisions, knowing more than your subordinates," and so on. Check it out and you will be amazed at how many unspoken values about management you can come up with.

Being in direct control of things all of the time is not the way we propose in this book that control be implemented. Also, having to know everything is definitely not a healthy assumption.

If your team must be self-reliant, would it be possible to know everything? No. So, if a team manager sticks to his previous belief system, he is probably an ineffective manager.

During a process of implementing teams, managers may get bruised so much that they learn it the hard way. But many top leaders never get to this. They implement team management and never contemplate the new values and belief systems that go with it. No one dares to raise the questions.

The consequence of this is that top management still evaluates managers on a values paradigm that no longer exists on the lower levels of the organization. This adds to the insurmountable squeeze that middle management is put into during the process.

One evening I had one of the internal instructors at my home to help him prepare a speech. He was going to tell about communication with his newly established self-directed work groups.

One particular point was that he did not want his middle managers to be converted into "delivery persons" between the groups and those who were going to communicate with them. In short, he wanted people to address group members directly in all matters that concerned them.

Then he added, "It would be nice to have people send me a copy for my information."

I looked intensely at him. He hesitated, and then continued: "...but on the other hand, I'll get the information I need directly from the group members."

After some additional reflection, he added: "Sometimes it's really difficult to leave such deep beliefs!"

–Finn

A few more things before we leave this subject.

Letting the team take responsibility means taking on tasks and responsibilities that were previously regarded as management jobs. This creates a fear of being displaced for many team leaders. Perhaps rightly so. After implementation of team-based management some organizations end up with fewer positions at the middle management level.

This is a relevant consideration. How can one expect a devoted employee to quickly and happily make himself or herself displaced? It is important to define the newly aligned role for managers during the process.

Equality and interest in other people is a major issue in teams.

A manager in charge of housekeeping at a larger facility was in her office. One of the employees came in and stated, "The cleaning girl in our department has not shown up."

The manager looked somewhat puzzled at her yet said nothing.

The employee then repeated, "The cleaning girl in our department — she has not shown up yet. What do you want us to do?"

The manager took her time, and then commented in a lowered voice, "The more I think of it, the more I come to the conclusion that we do not have any employee in the housekeeping department whose name is "The cleaning girl." Is it Ann we are talking about?"

"Yes, I assume it is. I really do not know."

"How long has Ann worked in your department?"

"I guess 1 1/2 years."

"What a shame you have not had the time to say hello to her yet!"

Last, people who take responsibility assume the right to create their own rules and competence for getting the job done. That means that ordinary agreements about working hours do not make sense the same way as they did before. Agreements with self-directed work teams are based more on congruent team behavior and aligned performance. That is not traditionally what's in a contract between the company and the employee.

If you implement a team-based organization, you'd better shift management beliefs and values as well.

Neglecting to implement Graves' "people" values might well spell disaster for the whole effort.

Chapter 9

Creating Empowerment

One day a frustrated manager came to me and described his problem: "I really believe in empowerment and input from employees, but the meetings to accomplish this last much too long!"

A few weeks later, I happened to be in an unrelated discussion with one of his employees. An unsolicited comment from the employee's perspective told the rest of the story: "When we have a meeting to discuss our department's work processes, it takes forever because the meeting cannot end until we all agree with the manager's point of view!"

I believe that the manager had the best of intentions and truly did not recognize his role in the situation. Unfortunately, his staff had identified the issue, but had chosen not to communicate directly with the manager in order to solve the problem.

–Arlene

Being empowered is one of the basics for being able to feel congruent. It might prove almost impossible if you are not allowed to use your full potential.

So creating an empowered state in the organization is a precondition for achieving true congruence and alignment.

9.1 Shadow Qualifications

WE ALL HAVE DIFFERENT IDENTITIES

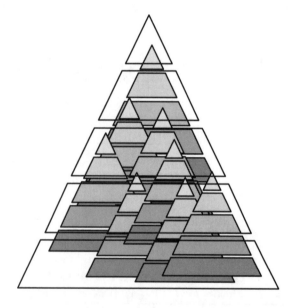

You probably recognize that very often people come home from educational experiences bringing valuable new insight to the company. Nevertheless, it's not being used. People become frustrated that they are not allowed to use all of their resources.

Actually, we all have different identities in life. Our professional identity is not the only aspect to our sense of self.

We have conducted many organizational diagnostics—asking people for their opinion on the issues in this book. One question stands out. Almost everybody tells us that they have personal resources that they do not use in their job—and that they would appreciate an opportunity to do so. We refer to these personal resources as "shadow qualifications."

One of our clients had a visitor from Russia. Not knowing that one of their employees had a Russian husband and spoke fluent Russian, they hired an interpreter.

At the last minute, they luckily discovered they had the expertise themselves.

One of our clients is an organization of social institutions that provides services to people with many different mental disabilities and physical handicaps.

They do not hire people on the basis of professional qualifications alone. They look consciously at shadow qualifications because other skills might also come in handy in getting the best quality of life for their patients.

Enabling people to use their full potential constitutes an opportunity to enforce personal congruence. This lowers tension between differing identities on and off the job. In addition, it gives the organization access to more resources.

The way to go about it is to ask. It's as simple as that. If you know more about people's potential, you bring yourself into a position to use it.

9.2 Power

Sharing power can be somewhat difficult. Why is that so? What are the beliefs that hold us back on this issue?

Many have the belief that sharing is giving away something you might have had for yourself. (The "theory of limited good!")

Think of it. What would be the most attractive management position for you? One where everybody is empowered and able to create results on their own? Or one where everybody does whatever you constitute as desired behavior?

For a majority, the first choice is probably what you desire. Why? Because personal power actually increases with the ability of your organization to produce results.

> *Letting go of power makes you more powerful.*

Could other assumptions interfere? Could it be that someone might be afraid of being outplayed by someone from a lower level in the organization? It could happen—no doubt about it.

Yes, we have seen people being replaced because of not making things in their organization work. Someone who helps his or her employees perform, however, is normally considered an attractive species.

The people you meet on your way up the organizational ladder may be the same ones you meet on your way down. There is no reason to be desperate because of the success of one of your employees. It might even prove valuable for you.

9.3 Getting the Insight

One morning one of our consultants arrived at a plant where he was to conduct employee training on company values and visions. He learned that they laid off 20 people the same morning.

Trying to convey a message of company values under these circumstances did not seem to be productive, so he contacted management to get an explanation.

> He learned that the particular part they had been producing had been outsourced. They simply had the opportunity to buy it cheaper elsewhere.
>
> But is that all there is to it?

It's not an unusual assumption that is shown by this action. One the surface, it sounds all right, but try to think about what assuptions might be behind it.

Being able to make a decision about outsourcing requires a minimum of insight into economic conditions. You must assume that these people knew both their own production costs and the alternative purchase price. You must assume that they have known it for a long time.

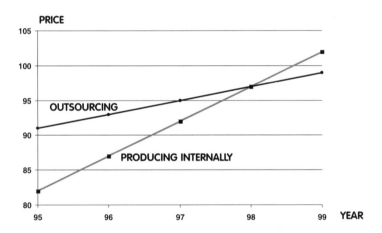

Making this assumption the picture that emerges is somewhat like above.

One might ask, what did management do during all these years when the economic feasibility of inhouse production deteriorated?

Apparently too little. It was bad management. But, in what way bad management?

The real lesson here is that if this information was shared with the involved employees, it might never have happened. Empowered employees would have taken the opportunity to save their jobs and save the company the money.

We are not putting moral judgment on any actions. However, if you choose the path of congruence and alignment (thereby making an assumption of trust in people) people would probably judge your organizational behavior incongruent if you fire people based on information they do not have. People do not normally align with organizations that make people redundant because of lack of involvement.

> *Empowering people by sharing information is not only necessary to create better results, it's the only way to make alignment work for you.*

Poster seen in the cafeteria:

"Without information there is no responsibility."

· Signed, The Management

Not a word was heard from management for the next three months.

9.4 The Right to Success and Failure

Have you heard about a manager "stealing" valuable work from employees and presenting it as his or her own? Probably yes.

It's almost obvious that this is not going to empower anyone. But it is less evident that the opposite is true as well. The right to account for one's own failures and being respected for it is equally important.

There are two major reasons for that.

The first one is the right to learn and get feedback. If I am in an environment where failures are covered up, practically all possibilities for learning are disrupted. Using failure as a learning opportunity is imperative if you want to seek congruence and alignment.

The second reason is that without failure almost all process is impossible. Does this sound strange? Not at all.

Actually, failure can be at least three different things. The normal failure—doing something **stupid** that you ought to know would lead to an undesirable result—this is number one. No doubt about it. That should be avoided. If you do fall into it, though, you'd better learn from it. That's the least you can do.

The second one is failure from **experimentation.** Experimenting leads inevitably to both success and failure. It's the path to development. If you want that, you'd better accept the failures that go with it.

The problem is, though, that all too often people do not realize the difference. That means that everything gets blame—even if a warranted risk leads to new insight. We have seen managers showing off with the normal gesture of telling everybody that in this organization they want people to make failures, forgetting that it was only the experimental ones they meant. It does not make sense or seem to be congruent when people nevertheless are blamed for the stupid ones.

> Finn plays tournament Bridge. It's a tough competition—playing 117 games on a weekend with your partner calls for concentration and accuracy on a very high level. No single card is played randomly. Every card has its own meaning and creates a pattern that constitutes the communication about strategy between partners.
>
> Making a mistake on this level almost immediately leads to internal grievance and self-blame.
>
> In your opinion, what would be the best reaction from a partner? Help, not blame, probably.

The third one is the one we label as the **professional** failure. That's the kind of failure you make as a professional and immediately know you did something wrong. It's like hanging on the edge of a cliff—holding on with just your fingers.

Taking action to blame this person is somewhat like stomping on this person's fingers and letting him drop into the valley. No blaming is called for—on the contrary. He needs a hand to help him draw himself up again.

Many managers are so fixed in their beliefs about their need to control and blame for failures they overlook the fact that this is almost the worst thing to do.

> *Empowerment means to abandon beliefs about your right and duty to blame for failure, your right and duty to place responsibility for mistakes, and your right and duty to credit success to the managers or the organization rather than the individual.*

Chapter 10

Values Revisited – Thoughts in the Logical Levels Perspective

Let's refer to values one last time. As this is the topic for the whole book, we will use this opportunity to just mention a few applications of the logical levels model, illustrating that the model can be used in many situations.

10.1 Annual Personnel Appraisals

One of the most painful and difficult practices conducted in organizations is the annual performance appraisal. It brings up images of checklists, rankings, and judgement. Issues of "rater error," "halo effect" and "contrast effect" lead to inaccuracies and ineffectiveness. They rarely produce lasting changed behavior.

Despite major changes in the nature of work, the performance appraisal process has not changed much over the years. Once-a-year discussions about behavior on an individual basis do not provide the most useful feedback.

Because of this, some companies have made the decision to abolish traditional reviews. Yet, there is a need for regular assessments.

One way to incorporate identity, values and beliefs, qualifications, and the environment (in addition to behavior) is to schedule an "annual alignment check."

Do the employee's logical levels match the organization's levels? What should be done about it over the next year?

ANNUAL CONGRUENCE AND ALIGNMENT TALKS

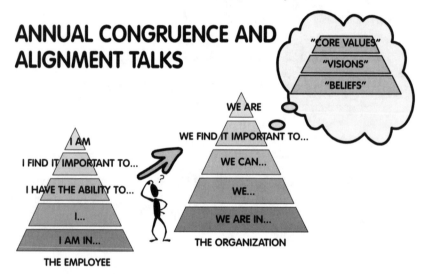

The procedure is carried out like this: Leadership, with input, makes decisions about the logical levels for the organization for the upcoming year. Core values would not change, but current strategic direction and required competence would be outlined. This determines what behavior is needed.

The conference between the employee and manager begins with the employee's carefully prepared logical levels. Managers ask about all the levels, and they agree on how to match that to the organization's needs.

Topics for discussion then become: Do the company values resonate with your personal values and beliefs? What do you want to learn be able to express them? What do you want to do? And, where do you want to do it?

These are relevant questions to ask of the leadership itself as well.

> *Personnel appraisals can be used to foster congruence and alignment.*

10.2 Recruitment

Alignment is critical for hiring decisions. In *Walk the Talk* by Lucia & Harvey they say:

> *Hire slowly and manage easily, or hire fast and manage with difficulty.*

LIMITED FOCUS WHEN HIRING

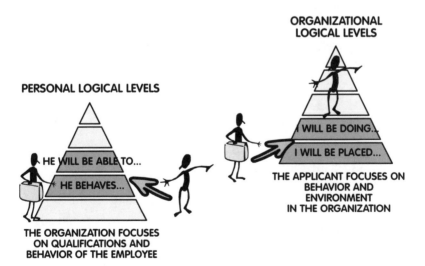

ORGANIZATIONAL
LOGICAL LEVELS

PERSONAL LOGICAL LEVELS

HE WILL BE ABLE TO...

HE BEHAVES...

THE ORGANIZATION FOCUSES
ON QUALIFICATIONS AND
BEHAVIOR OF THE EMPLOYEE

I WILL BE DOING...

I WILL BE PLACED...

THE APPLICANT FOCUSES ON
BEHAVIOR AND
ENVIRONMENT
IN THE ORGANIZATION

Many ads for new staff focus solely on qualifications and behavior. Not many include professional values.

The model on the previous page illustrates that both parties might have a focus that is too narrow. The logical thing to do, of course, is to focus systematically on all of the levels.

As a company, we created an ad for a new accountant by using values terminology such as, "You appreciate... You value ... You feel good about..."

We got many fine applicants. Several said they felt something was unusual in the ad. They could not spot what it was!

Changing values in employees after they have joined you is more difficult than adding qualifications if the values are in sync.

10.3 Conflict Resolution

Many conflicts arise because of behavioral misunderstandings. Here is a procedure that we recommend.

The first thing to agree on is what the conflict is about—the symptoms that are obvious to everyone.

Both parties must agree on the criteria for success in this situation —what is going to be acceptable for both. Win/win would often be a preferred concept, but as we know now, different cultural paradigms might value different solutions.

The third phase is to clarify the "maps of the world." This means trying to understand whatever the other person's point of view is, regardless of your own map. This is where the crucial questions: "How can it possibly be so?" and "What's important about that?" come into play. This brings an understanding of the deeper structure of the conflict. The logical levels enter here. On what level do we have to solve this? Is it really a matter of values? Is it a matter of identity? Or, is it purely behavior?

> Once in a business negotiation, I reached the lowest day when the opponent "threatened" me (my perception) about the "trouble" I was about to be in if I did not follow his suggestions.
>
> I knew we had to focus on higher levels again. I contacted him and said basically, "Neither of us wants this to be how it is—please tell me again what is really important for you in all of this? What are you trying to do?" He outlined three values: to be recognized, to get a new start, and to preserve our relationship. It gave us a productive direction. We settled everything the next day. By having this discussion, it reminded both of us about what was truly important.
>
> *–Arlene*

We could illustrate it like this:

CONFLICT RESOLUTION

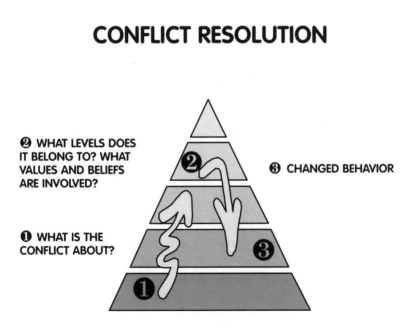

❷ WHAT LEVELS DOES IT BELONG TO? WHAT VALUES AND BELIEFS ARE INVOLVED?

❸ CHANGED BEHAVIOR

❶ WHAT IS THE CONFLICT ABOUT?

Phase	Content
The issue	The apparent conflict
Success criteria	Agree about what type of solution you want (win/win, expedient, etc.)
Statement of views	Exchanging the "Map of the World" about the relationship between exposed behavior and intentions ***How can it possibly be so?*** ***What's important about that?***
Logical level we disagree on	***Behavior, qualifications or values***
Possibilities	Create possible solutions
Evaluate	What possibilities meet the criteria and the values we try to meet?
Deal	What do we do from here?
Learning	What did we learn from this?

10.4 Coaching

One day an old man moved into town. The old man was carving stones, only moving small parts at a time with great caution.

One of the local boys became interested and slipped quietly into a corner to see the old man working. It was amazing. The old man seemed to have endless hours in front of him, yet he did not lose his concentration.

After some time the boy gathered his courage and asked the old man, "What's your name?"

The old man answered, "My name is Michelangelo."

The boy continued, "What are you doing?"

> The old man looked at him with his mild eyes and answered, "I am freeing the angel inside the stone."

Coaching is really about freeing the angel inside of others. Basically, coaching in management is as much a technique as a style. **Technically**, it's a process by which the coach, through a series of questions, enables the coached person to realize and solve his or her own problems and possibilities.

As a management style, **coaching** enables the employees to solve their own problems. Employees are not pushed into solutions they have not worked out for themselves.

It goes without saying that coaching as a style and a technique is ideally suited for creating congruence and alignment.

Coaching can be used to solve a problem or to set challenging goals. We normally use a procedure we learned from John Withmore's book, *Coaching for Performance*. It uses an acronym of **GROW: G**oals, **R**ealities, **O**ptions and **W**ill.

COACHING

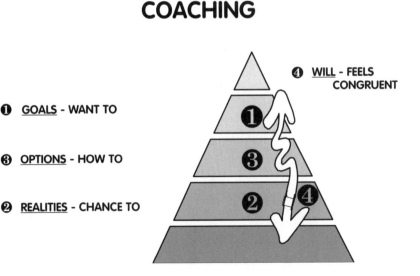

❶ <u>GOALS</u> - WANT TO

❸ <u>OPTIONS</u> - HOW TO

❷ <u>REALITIES</u> - CHANCE TO

❹ <u>WILL</u> - FEELS CONGRUENT

The coach asks questions in each of the four areas. Discussion moves from helping the coached person form goals, check reality, form solutions for reaching the goals, and finally checking within himself whether he feels up to it. By using each of the levels, it becomes a process for congruence.

The trick is only to ask questions, never to suggest solutions. You must keep your own opinion out of it. The skill is also to listen carefully to any sign of limiting factors that might prevent the person from reaching the goal.

Let's look at limiting factors—what could they be? They could be limiting factors on any of the levels: outside factors in the environment, lack of behavioral possibilities, lack of competence to do what's required for the solution, or limiting belief systems.

> *One way to structure a coaching session is to ask questions on each of the logical levels. By doing so, you enable the person to create a congruent solution for himself or herself.*

This is an internal decision-making process that you create for the coached person. The same process can also work in other contexts.

When a **decision** must be made, try to isolate the different levels of the decision. What values are going to be expressed? What are the realities? Do we have the competence for the solution? Finally, does it feel good?

In **negotiations,** use the same model. Go for the values first. You will get a much more lasting result by addressing alignment for both of the parties on values as well as behavioral levels.

Chapter 11

Committing to New Beliefs

11.1 The Power of Beliefs

For me efficiency is of high value, not the least when it comes to keeping the home. By this token you would probably agree that running out of dishes before the dishwasher is full is really devastating—having to take dirty dishes out and wash them. The remedy, of course, is to buy a full load of dishes.

So, some time ago I was washing my cheesecutter by hand and came to think that this was really foolish. I went down and bought another five—never to wash them by hand again.

I began to use this story in my workshops as an example of values-driven improvement. But one day one of the participants said: (no kidding) "I have two baskets. One is placed in the drawer. In this way I do not even have to empty the basket."

I was impressed. Then, in my next course someone said: (no kidding) "I have two dishwashers. I do not even have to move the basket." — *Finn*

Maybe you smile ...but the power of values in this story is exactly the power many have searched for and never achieved in their quality improvement programs.

> **Knowledge and insight are the shortest routes to your goals.**

11.2 The "Prince" of Insight

Did you dare to kiss the frog? Did you read this book and reorganize some of your beliefs? If so, with your "princely" new insights, you can transform values into action.

What beliefs did you reorganize?

Here are some points you might have accepted during your reading.

You might have contemplated that your firm belief in strategic planning (based on cause and effect) is more doubtful than you previously realized. Many things cannot be planned or anticipated. Direct control does not lead to commitment, creativity, adaptability, flexibility, and people's personal contributions. To get to the heart of that you have to consider congruence and alignment as basic principles for leadership. This is a different approach to control. Remember:

> **Motivation, change, adaptability, flexibility, complexity, networking, and so on are not achieved through traditional behavioral control but by the power of congruence and alignment.**

You might have realized that much more depends on values and beliefs than you previously took into account. Cultural paradigms and belief systems in many cases have been the hidden factors that you did not take into consideration when you planned a major campaign. That's why some of them failed.

> **Trying to implement tools that have no support in the present value systems of the organization is fruitless.**

You might have valued the simple approach of the logical levels as a tool for a lot of different issues—from complicated change processes like mergers and acquisitions to day-to-day problems like creating understanding, self-esteem, team building, recruitment, personnel appraisals, conflict resolution and many more. You may have reorganized some of your beliefs in other approaches based merely on behavior.

> **Don't forget to ask:**
> - **"How can it possibly be so?"**
> - **"What is important about that?"**
>
> **This will give you the key to creating commitment.**

During your reading you might even have considered your own personal congruence and that of your organization. It may have created a higher awareness of changes needed for yourself and the organization to create a congruent and aligned culture.

Many other beliefs were expressed in the book. During your reading you might even have done away with some of your own limiting beliefs.

Have you transformed the "frog" of your limiting beliefs into the "prince" of new insight?

> "I know you can fight, but it's your mind that makes you a man."
> *— from the movie "Braveheart"*

Definitions

Here are some of the basic definitions and characteristics of concepts and words that are used in the book.

Basic Concepts :	Definition and Characteristics:
Learning Organization	A Learning Organization is one that puts a focus on internal learning through: • Creating possibilities to learn (Time, technology, systems and organization) • Creating an environment for learning (The seven disciplines) • Creating a leadership style that focuses on learning (qualification level in logical levels of change)
Values-Based Management	Values-Based Management is a leadership style focusing on control by addressing higher logical levels. The basic concept is to: • Create congruence for the individual and for the organization • Create alignment between the individual and the organization
Values	Values represent inner states that we desire. Values are key elements in achieving internal congruence and external alignment.
Alignment	Alignment is bringing one set of logical levels into harmony with another – such as an individual to an organization.

Basic Concepts :	Definition and Characteristics:
Congruence	Congruence is bringing all logical levels of one entity (an individual or an organization) in harmony
Levels of Values	**Core-values** are unchanging over time **Visions** relate to business goals and direction **Beliefs** are day-to-day values—rules and preferences—that we apply in day-to-day decision-making
Leadership	Leadership is directing the organization to future attractive states. Leadership is addressing the higher logical levels of values, identity, and qualifications.
Management	Management is administrating resources. Management then becomes controlling at the behavior and environment level
Who is controlling?	Controlling the business is a management responsibility. No attempt to rethink control disputes that.
Map of the World	The personal perspective of the "real" world. One particular important context in Values-Based Management is one's (unwarranted) map of certain "true" relationships between behavior and values/beliefs.
Process communication	Communication on all logical levels.
Manipulation	To behave incongruently in relation to (hidden) objectives.

Basic Concepts :	Definition and Characteristics:
Group	A group is a gathering of people with relatively few relationships – individuals reacting to problems on an individual basis
Team	A team is a group of people who have established excellent professional relationships of trust between each other. This enables the team to respond to problems as a unit, making the most of each member's contribution.
Team-Based Management	Team-based management is a leadership style focusing on creating teams and maintaining their high efficiency. Characteristics are: • drawing focus away from the behavior level and focusing on qualifications and values • the manager normally is not a team member • no hierarchical structure is established in the team
Empowerment	Is, among other things, the right to: • use one's competencies • participate • get insight in data • get access to resources • decide when one has the best information to do the task or make the decision • be accountable and receive credit for one's own successes and failures

Other related Concepts :	Definition and Characteristics:
Coaching individuals	Is a planned session where the goal is to enable the coached person to release his or her full potential. Characteristics include: • it's planned and aside from the "heat of battle" of the real working situation • the coach keeps his/her own beliefs and values to him or herself • it's (among other things) based on structured questioning techniques
Coaching of Teams	Collective coaching with the purpose of getting the team to release its full potential. It involves different techniques from individual coaching. Coaching of teams is a tool for team-based management.
Coach	One who performs individual coaching. Used in our concept as a management role, not as a position in the organization.
Coaching management style	Is a management style focusing on letting people find their own answers. No directive advice is given.
Process consultant / facilitator	One who takes care of team/group processes. Characteristics would be: • It occurs while the team is working • It's based on interventions such as observations or suggestions for better processes or communication. • It's based on an agreement with the team. • The role can be performed by someone external to the team as well as group members themselves.

Other related Concepts :	Definition and Characteristics:
Advisor	One who gives advice based on particular expert knowledge of the problem
Supervision	Is to observe a process in order to give feedback. Characteristics are: • It's for the benefit of the supervised; it's not an evaluation for some third party. • The supervisor shares his or her observations with the supervised. • Feedback can be agreed upon to be at many levels—from observation to evaluation and interpretation.

The pool

Here is the "mental jogging" example.

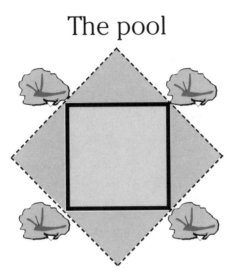

The pool

Some of the solutions could be:

1. Turn it 45 degrees!

2. Make it double depth.

3. Make it some other place and fill the old one.

4. Make four small islands of trees.

5. Remove the trees to some other location.

Did you discover more?

Literature

The Learning Organization

Champy, James. *Reengineering Management*. Harper Business, 1995.

Dydan, Gordon, and Dr. Jeannette Vos. *The Learning Revolution*. Accelerated Learning Systems, Ltd., 1994.

Kline, Peter and Bernhard Saunders. *Ten Steps to a Learning Organization*. Great Ocean Publishers, 1993.

Mayo, Andrew and Elisabeth Lank. *The Power of Learning*. IPD House, 1994.

Neergaard, Claus, Finn van Hauen and Bjarne Kastberg. *Den Lærende Organisation* i Praksis. Industriens Forlag, 1997. (Danish).

Senge, Peter. *The Fifth Discipline: The Art and Practice of The Learning Organization*. Doubleday, 1990.

Senge, Peter, Charlotte Roberts, Richard B. Ross, Bryan J. Smith & Art Kleiner. *The Fifth Discipline Fieldbook*. Nicolas Brealey Publishing, 1994.

Swieringa, Joop and André Wierdsma. *Becoming a Learning Organization*. Addison-Wesley Publishing Company, 1992.

van Hauen, Finn, Vagn Strandgaard and Bjarne Kastberg. *Den Lærende Organisation*. Industriens Forlag, 1995. (Danish).

Values-Based Management

Beck, Don Edward, and Christopher C. Cowan. *Spiral Dynamics: Mastering Values, Leadership, and Change*. Blackwell Publishers, 1996.

Cohen, Ben and Jerry Greenfield. *Ben & Jerry's Double-Dip – Lead With Your Values and Make Money, Too*. Simon & Schuster, 1997.

Collins, James and Jerry Porras. *Built to Last.* Harper Business, 1994.

Covey, Steven R. *Principle-Centered Leadership.* Summit Books, 1990/1991.

Harvey, Eric and Alexander Lucia. *Walk the Talk ... and Get the Results You Want.* Performance Publishing Company, 1995.

Keeney, Ralph L. *Value focused Thinking, A Path to Creative Decision making.* Harward University Press, 1992.

Kouzes, James M. and Barry Z. Posner. *Credibility.* Jossey-Bass Inc., 1993.

Lebow, Rob and William Simon. *Lasting Change.* Van Nostrand Reinhold, 1997.

Lebow, Rob. *A Journey into the Heroic Environment.* Prima Publishing, 1997.

O'Toole, James. Leading Change, *The Argument for Value-Based Leadership.* Jossey-Bass, Inc., 1995.

van Hauen, Finn, Bjarne Kastberg, Mette Denager, Egil Hjertaker og Karin Hjertaker. *Værdier på Jobbet.* Industriens Forlag 1997. (Danish).

Virtual or Complex Organizations

Greiner, Ray and George Metes. *Going Virtual.* Prentice Hall, 1995.

Hale, Richard and Peter Whitlam. *Towards The Virtual Organization.* McGraw-Hill, 1997.

Hedberg, Bo, Göran Dahlgren, Jörgen Hansson and Nils-Göran Olve. *Virtual Organizations and Beyond.* John Wiley & Sons, Inc., 1994, 1998.

Henry, James and Meg Hartzler. *Tools for Virtual Teams.* ASQ Quality Press, 1998.

Jones, Larry and Chuka Mui: *Unleashing the Killer App.*

Kelly, Kevin. *Out of Control.* Addison Wesley Publishing Company, 1994.

Lipnack, Jessica and Jeffrey Stamps. *Virtual Teams*. John Wiley & Sons, Inc.,1997.

Sanders, Irene. *Strategic Thinking and the New Science*. The Free Press, 1998.

Wheatley, Margaret J. *Leadership and the New Science*. Berrett-Koehler Publishers, 1992.

Zohar, Danah and Ian Marshall. *The Quantum Society: Mind, Physics, and a New Social Revolution*. William Morrow and Company, 1994.

Learning / Teaching / Neurolinguistic Programming (NLP)

Campbell, Linda, Bruce Campell, and Dee Dickinson. *Teaching & Learning Through Multiple Intelligences*. Allyn & Bacon, 1996.

Dilts, Robert. *Application of Neuro-Linguistic Programming*. Meta Publications, 1983.

Gardner, Howard. *Frames of Mind*. BasicBooks. 1983, 1992.

Hjertaker, Egil. *Læring gjennom samarbeid*. Tano, 1984/1990.

Jensen, Eric. *Superteaching*. Turning Point for Teachers, 1988.

Jensen, Eric. *The Learning Brain*. Turning Point for Teachers, 1994.

Knight, Sue. *NLP at Work*. Nicholas Brealey Publishing, 1995.

Kolb, D.A. *Experimental Learning*. Prentice Hall, Englewood Cliffs, 1984.

Lazear, David. *Seven Ways of Teaching*. IRI SkyLight, 1991.

Nyhand, Barry. *Developing People's Ability to Learn*. European Interuniversity Press, 1991.

Strandgaard, Vagn, Finn van Hauen and Bjarne Kastberg. *Aktiviteter for undervisning I+II – instruktørstøtteværktøjer for Den Lærende Organisation*. Industriens Forlag, 1995.

Other Management

Chaize, Jacques. *Døren til forandring åbnes indefra.* Forlaget Ankerhus og Danfoss A/S, 1994. (Danish).

Nelson, Robert B. *Powering Employees Through Delegation.* 1994.

Nirenberg, John. *The Living Organization.* Pfeiffer, 1993.

Smonhouse, Clarke. *Rethinking the Company.* 1994.

Withmore, John. *Coaching for Performance.* Nicolas Brealey, 1992.

Teamwork / Teambuilding / Meetings

Belbin, Meridith. *Team Roles at Work.* Butterwoth, Heinemann, 1993.

Fisher, Kimball and Mareen Duncan Fisher. *The Distributed Mind: Achieving High Performance Through the Collective Intelligence of Knowledge Work Teams.* American Management Association, AMACOM, 1998.

Strandgaard, Vagn, Finn van Hauen and Bjarne Kastberg. *Det samarbejdende menneske – teambuilding for Den Lærende Organization.* Industriens Forlag, 1995.

Strandgaard, Vagn, Finn van Hauen and Bjarne Kastberg. *Aktiviteter for teambuilding – instruktørstøtteværktøjer for Den lærende Organization.* Industriens Forlag, 1995.

Self-Esteem

Branden, Nathaniel. *The Six Pillars of Self-Esteem.* Bantam, 1994.

Cameron, Julia. *The Artist's Way: A Spiritual Path to Higher Creativity.* G.P.Putnam's Sons, 1992.

Canfield, Jack. *Chicken Soup for the Soul.* Heath Communications Inc., 1993 (And subsequent publications in the series.)

Covey, Steven R. *The 7 Habits of Highly Effective People.* Simon and Schuster, 1989.

Covey, Steven R. *First Things First.* Simon and Schuster, 1994.

Davies, Phillippa. *Total Confidence.* Piatkus, 1994.

Frey, Diane and C. J. Carlock. *Enhancing Self Esteem.* Accelerated Development Inc., 1989.

Palladino, Connie D. *Developing Self Esteem: A Positive Guide for Personal Success.* Kogan Page, 1989, 1993.

Steinem, Gloria. *Selvværd. Den Indre Revolution.* Munksgaard, 1992. (Danish).

van Hauen, Finn, Bjarne Kastberg and Vagn Strandgaard. *Dig og dine skjulte ressourcer.* Industriens Forlag, 1997. (Danish).